westermann

NOTTING HILL GATE

Arbeitsbuch Inklusion 6

Erarbeitet von:
Gisela Ehlers (Schillsdorf) und Martin Weber (Wiesbaden)

Fachliche Beratung:
Prof. Dr. David Gerlach (Wuppertal)

Notting Hill Gate 6
Arbeitsbuch Inklusion

Materialien zu Notting Hill Gate 6

Für Lehrkräfte:

- Textbook für Lehrkräfte 6 (ISBN 978-3-14-128285-6)
- Materialien für Lehrkräfte 6 (ISBN 978-3-14-128295-5)
- Lernerfolgskontrollen 6 (ISBN 978-3-14-128321-1)
- CD für Lehrkräfte 6 (ISBN 978-3-14-128305-1)
- DVD für Lehrkräfte 6 (ISBN 978-3-14-128315-0)
- Online-Diagnose zu Notting Hill Gate 6
  www.onlinediagnose.de

Für Schülerinnen und Schüler:

- Textbook 6 (ISBN 978-3-14-128201-6)
- Workbook 6 (inkl. Audios) (ISBN 978-3-14-128211-5)
- Interaktive Übungen 6 (WEB-14-128221)
- Klassenarbeitstrainer 6 (ISBN 978-3-14-128247-4)
- Grammatiktrainer 6 (ISBN 978-3-14-128387-7)
- Wortschatztrainer 6 (ISBN 978-3-14-128241-2)

Das digitale Schulbuch und digitale Unterrichtsmaterialien für Schülerinnen und Schüler und für Lehrkräfte finden Sie in der BiBox – dem digitalen Unterrichtssystem passend zum Lehrwerk. Mehr Informationen über aktuelle Lizenzen finden Sie auf www.bibox.schule.

www.westermann.de/nhg

DIGITAL+

Alle digitalen Ergänzungen zum Buch erkennen Sie an dem Symbol **DIGITAL+**.
Dazu zählen Audiotracks, Videoclips und Arbeitsblätter zur Medienbildung.
Gehen Sie auf **www.westermann.de/webcode** und geben Sie den Webcode **WES-128231-001** ein.
Sie können auch den QR-Code scannen.

Druck A[1] / Jahr 2023
Alle Drucke der Serie A sind im Unterricht parallel verwendbar.

Redaktion: Doris Bos
Illustrationen: Mario Ellert, Bremen
Umschlaggestaltung: LIO Design GmbH, Braunschweig
Layout: LIO Design GmbH, Braunschweig
Druck und Bindung: Westermann Druck GmbH, Braunschweig

ISBN 978-3-14-**128231**-3

So arbeitest du mit dem Buch

DIGITAL+

Alle digitalen Ergänzungen zum Buch erkennst du an dem Symbol **DIGITAL+**.
Dazu zählen Audiotracks, Videoclips und Arbeitsblätter zur Medienbildung.
Gehe auf www.westermann.de/webcode
und gib den Webcode WES-128231-001 ein.
Du kannst auch den QR-Code scannen.

Bei den Aufgaben findest du folgende Verweise:

1 audio	Zu dieser Aufgabe gibt es einen Audiotrack.
2 video	Zu dieser Aufgabe gibt es einen Videoclip.
3 DIGITAL+	Dieses Symbol kennzeichnet Aufgaben, in denen du Medienkompetenz aufbaust und trainierst. Hierzu gibt es ein Arbeitsblatt.
TARGET TASK	In der Target Task (Zielaufgabe) wendest du an, was du gelernt hast. Du erarbeitest ein kleines Produkt, das du in der Klasse vorstellen und in deinem Portfolio aufbewahren kannst.

Hier findest du Tipps. !

Wörter in **grauer Schrift** kannst du in deinen eigenen Sätzen austauschen.

Welcome!

Auf dieser Seite kannst du ein Quiz machen und dein Arbeitsbuch kennenlernen. Wenn du den Buchstaben bei der richtigen Antwort einkreist und unten einträgst, erhältst du das Lösungswort.
Viel Spaß mit Notting Hill Gate!

1 Welche *Unit* beginnt auf Seite 55?

(R) *Unit* 5
(H) *Unit* 3

2 Wovon handelt *Unit* 2, *Part* A?

(O) Von Festen und Traditionen
(A) Von London

3 Was beginnt auf Seite 148?

(L) Der Vokabelanhang
(R) *Unit* 5

4 Was ist auf Seite 137?

(Y) Die *Wordbank Wildlife*
(I) Die *Wordbank Good style*

5 Was steht auf Seite 102?

(W) *Practise More* von *Unit* 4
(D) Die Seite *Important Words* von Unit 4

6 Wo findest du eine Liste von Zahlen?

(A) Auf Seite 127
(O) Auf Seite 129

7 Was steht in *Unit* 5, *Part* B?

(Y) Eine Gespenstergeschichte
(O) Ein Märchen

8 Was beginnt auf Seite 7?

(K) *Unit* 2
(S) *Unit* 1

1	2	3	4	5	6	7	8

Welcome back to Notting Hill!

London

Ava Kogan

- 12 years old
- lives with her mum, her dad and her two brothers Joshua and Noah
- has a dog, Ollie
- likes skateboarding
- goes to the book club at school
- her grandmother Edyta lives in Poland

Lily and Harry Norris

- 12 years old
- live with their mums, Olivia and Sarah
- have two rabbits
- like playing board games
- Lily: goes to the science club and the book club at school
- Harry: plays the guitar in the school band

Tarek Adil

- 13 years old
- lives with his dad
- has an uncle, Sami
- likes cooking and playing football
- goes to the cooking club at school

1

Holidays

1 Look at the pictures. Where are the people?
2 What are the people doing?
3 What is your favourite picture?

Part A Holiday fun

- Du erfährst, was manche Kinder in den Ferien gemacht haben.
- Du lernst, über Vergangenes zu sprechen.
- Du schreibst etwas über Ferien in einem Blog.

Part B Sightseeing in London

- Du lernst Sehenswürdigkeiten in London kennen.
- Du übst Wegbeschreibungen.
- Du planst einen Tag in London.
- Du erstellst eine Seite für einen Reiseführer.

Holiday activities

1a

Match the sentences to the photos. Ordnet die Sätze den Fotos zu.

☐ 

☐ 

1 The adventure park was lots of fun.

2 In the holidays I went to the USA.
We hiked every day.

3 We did a lot of sightseeing in Paris.

4 My holidays at the seaside were fantastic.
We often played beach volleyball.

☐ 

1 

1b audio 1

Listen to the statements and read along. Match two of the photos to the texts.
Hört euch die Aussagen an und lest mit. Verbindet zwei der Fotos mit den Texten.

A Hi, I'm Sarah. In the holidays I stayed at home. One day my parents took me to an adventure park. It was a lot of fun!

B My name is George. I went abroad in the holidays. I went to the USA by plane with my brother, my dad and my grandpa. We hiked every day in the Rocky Mountains. It was fantastic! The views from the mountaintops were spectacular.

1c

Tell a partner what you like doing in the holidays. Take turns.
Erzähle einem Partner / einer Partnerin, was du gern in den Ferien machst. Wechselt einander ab.

I like …

going to the beach

staying at home

going sightseeing

doing sports

meeting friends

playing video games

going swimming

riding my bike

The children's holidays

2a

Read the text messages. Where are Tarek and Ava?
Lies die Textnachrichten. Wo sind Tarek und Ava?

4friends

Ava Hi guys! How are you all? I'm still at my grandma's in Poland.
Last week I went riding. I had a very lazy horse.
But it was fun.

5:10pm

Tarek I arrived at Green Farm in Wales on Friday. It's great here! 5:13pm

Lily What did you say before you left? "Farms are sooooo boring!" 5:14pm

Tarek I didn't say that, Lily. 😉 Yesterday I milked a cow for the first time in my life, and I liked it. And I was really good at it! Later we had fresh milkshakes. Yummy! 5:15pm

4friends

Lily Haha, that sounds like fun! Did your dad take a picture? 5:15pm

Tarek No, he didn't. He didn't have time. He milked his own cow.

5:13pm

Harry Aren't you afraid of cows, Tarek? 5:17pm

Tarek No, I'm not. I also went cycling two days ago. And now it's dinner time for the chickens. Talk to you later! Video chat at 7pm? 5:18pm

2b

Read again. Complete the sentences and write them down.
Lies noch einmal. Vervollständige die Sätze und schreibe sie auf.

??? went riding. Ava went riding.

??? arrived in Wales on Friday.

??? and ??? milked cows.

??? went cycling two days ago.

2c

Talk about what you think about holidays on a farm. Sprecht darüber, was ihr von Ferien auf einem Bauernhof haltet.

I think holidays on a farm are boring / fun / ...

I like ...

GRAMMAR HELP

Wenn du über etwas sprechen willst, das in der Vergangenheit liegt, verwendest du die einfache Vergangenheit *(simple past)*. Sieh dir die Beispiele an.

Einige Verben erhalten die Endung *-ed* an ihre Grundform, z. B.: stay – stay**ed**

I stay**ed** at home in the holidays. I lik**ed** it.
She visit**ed** Paris.
We work**ed** on the farm.

Einige Verben haben unregelmäßige Formen, die du lernen musst, z. B.: go – **went**, do – **did**

I **went** to London and **took** a lot of photos.
She **did** her homework.
They **had** a hamburger.

Uncle Sami's Holidays

3

What did Uncle Sami do (+) or not do (–) in the holidays? Write sentences. **Was hat Onkel Sami im Urlaub gemacht (+) oder nicht gemacht (–)? Schreibe Sätze.**

+

ate · took · stayed · visited · ~~went~~

Uncle Sami ______went______ (go) to Italy.
He ____________ (stay) in a hotel.
He ____________ (visit) Rome.
He ____________ (eat) Italian food.
He ____________ (take) photos.

–

do · ~~go~~ · milk · work

Uncle Sami **didn't** ______go______ to France.
He **didn't** ____________ a cow.
Uncle Sam **didn't** ____________
He **didn't** ____________ sports.

How to say the letters -ed

4 audio 2

Listen to the words and read along. Then repeat them. **Höre dir die Wörter an und lies mit. Wiederhole sie dann.**

worked · stayed · visited · hiked · loved · started · looked · arrived · wanted · liked · played · collected

A video chat

5a audio 3

Listen to the video chat and read along. What are the children talking about?
Höre dir den Videochat an und lies mit. Worüber sprechen die Kinder?

It's 7pm. The children are on a video chat.
Harry: Hi guys – nice to see you all!
Tarek: Hey, how are you? What did you do last week?
Harry: We renovated Lily's new room. Lily moved her stuff last weekend.
Tarek: What did you do with Double and Trouble? Did they move to Lily's room, too?
Harry: No, they didn't. One week they live with Lily, and the next week they live with me.
Ava: Good idea. Did you do anything else?
Lily: Yes, we did. We cycled a lot, and we had a picnic in the garden.
Harry: And we went to the Museum of London.
Tarek: Were you in London all the time?
Harry: No, we weren't. We visited our grandparents in Bristol for a couple of days.
Lily: When are you guys back in London? I could show you all my new room.
Ava: Great idea! What about next Saturday?
Tarek: See you next Saturday then.

5b

What did Harry and Lily do in the holidays? Fill in the missing words. **Was haben Harry und Lily in den Ferien gemacht? Trage die fehlenden Wörter ein.**

Harry and Lily ______________________ Lily's new room.

Lily ______________________ her stuff last weekend.

They ______________________ a picnic in the garden.

They ______________________ to the Museum of London.

They ______________________ their grandparents in Bristol.

5c

Ask and answer questions with a partner.
Stellt einem Partner / einer Partnerin Fragen und beantwortet sie.

Did Harry and Lily renovate *Ava's room*?

Did they go to the *park*?

Did they visit their *grandparents*?

Did they have a *picnic*?

Yes, they did.

No, they didn't.

Back in Notting Hill

6a

Tarek took some pictures on his holiday in Wales. What can you see?
Tarek hat ein paar Bilder in seinem Urlaub in Wales gemacht. Was kannst du sehen?

Cardiff Castle · a roundhouse · signs in English and Welsh

I can see …

6b audio 4

Listen and read along. What is Tarek talking about? Tick. ✓
Höre zu und lies mit. Worüber spricht Tarek? Mache ein Häkchen.

☐ He is talking about Cardiff Castle and shopping in Cardiff.

☐ He is talking about Cardiff Castle, the Welsh Folk Museum and the Welsh language.

Harry: Tarek, how were the last days of your holiday in Wales?
Tarek: After our week on the farm, my dad and I went to Cardiff. It was great. We went to Cardiff Castle and the Welsh Folk Museum.
Lily: What was that like?
Tarek: The Welsh Folk Museum is an open-air museum. There is a roundhouse that shows how people lived two thousand years ago.
Ava: And how did you like the castle? What did you do there?
Tarek: We went on a guided tour. The guide was really cool. Did you know that the Romans first built a fort there?
Lily: Phew, thank you for the history lesson, Tarek. Did you learn any words in Welsh?
Tarek: Yes, I did. For example, Wales is "Cymru" in Welsh.

6c

Read the text again. Underline the information about the museum in red and about the castle in blue. **Lies den Text noch einmal. Unterstreiche die Informationen über das Museum in Rot und über die Burg in Blau.**

Catching up with Ellen

7a

Look at the pictures. What did Ellen do in the holidays?

Sieh dir die Bilder an. Was hat Ellen in den Ferien gemacht?

7b audio 5

Then listen to Lily and Ellen on the phone and point to the matching pictures.

Höre dann Lily und Ellen am Telefon zu und zeige auf die passenden Bilder.

7c audio 5

Now listen again and number the pictures.

Höre nun noch einmal zu und nummeriere die Bilder.

7d

Read the questions. Find the correct answers and write them down.

Lies die Fragen. Finde die richtigen Antworten und schreibe sie auf.

Where did Ellen spend her holidays? *She was in Spain.*

Who was with her? ______

Where was her hotel? ______

What did she do every day? ______

What did she eat at a small restaurant? ______

She swam in the sea. · ~~She was in Spain.~~ · She ate tapas. · It was near the beach. · Her parents and her brother.

How was your last holiday?

8

Walk around the classroom. Ask and answer questions.

Lauft im Klassenzimmer herum. Stellt Fragen und beantwortet sie.

How was your last holiday?

It was …

great · cool · exciting · …

What did you do?

I …

stayed at home · visited … · went to the park · went swimming a lot · played … · …

Blog posts about the holidays

9a

Look at the pictures. What did the people do in the holidays?
Sieh dir die Bilder an. Was haben die Leute in den Ferien gemacht?

played football · went to the swimming pool · did the cooking · went for long walks · saw friends · went to the park · went to a summer camp · played board games · made some salad · did arts and crafts · …

9b

Read the blog post. Where did Philipp spend his holidays?
Lies den Blogpost. Wo hat Philipp seine Ferien verbracht?

https://www.blogname.co.uk/holidays × –

Hello there! I hope you all enjoyed your holidays. I stayed at home this year. My mum and dad went to work every day, and I looked after my two brothers. We had a lot of fun together. We often went to the park near our house. Some of our friends were also at home, so we could meet them there and play football. One day we went to the swimming pool, and one rainy day we went to the cinema.

Philipp, 15

Roddy on 23rd August at 11:24am said:
I also stayed at home, and I think holidays at home are brilliant! Thanks for writing about yours!

9c

Copy the text and fill in the gaps with words from the box. Schreibe den Text ab und fülle die Lücken mit Wörtern aus dem Kasten aus.

brothers · cinema · play · ~~stayed~~ · went · went

Philipp ??? at home for the holidays this year. His parents ??? to work every day, and he looked after his two ???. He and his brothers ??? to the park near their house to ??? football with their friends. One rainy day they went to the ???.

Philipp stayed at home for ____________________

____

____

____

____

____

Holidays

11a

Read the poem about holidays. How many words has it got?
Lies das Gedicht über Ferien. Wie viele Wörter hat es?

Holidays
free time
really long drive
hotel by the sea
happiness

11b

Write a poem with eleven words about your holidays.
Schreibe ein Gedicht mit elf Wörtern über deine Ferien.

Think of a place:
hotel, campsite, caravan, home, ...

Think of the people:
parents, brothers, sisters, grandpa, ...

____

________ ________

________ ________ ________

________ ________ ________ ________

____

Think of the weather:
sunny, rainy, cold, hot, ...

Think of activities:
do sports, play ..., visit ...

What did they do?

12a

Complete the text with the verb forms from the box.
Vervollständige den Text mit den Verbformen aus dem Kasten.

had · went · didn't stay · wasn't · liked · visited

In the holidays, Ava's grandparents w__ __ __ to Bristol.

They __ __ __ __ ' t __ __ __ __ in a hotel, but in a B&B.

On their last day they __ __ __ __ __ __ __ an art museum.

Then they __ __ __ dinner in a small restaurant.

Ava's grandma __ __ __ __ __ the food very much, but her grandfather thought it __ __ __ __ ' __ very nice.

12b

Compare with a partner. **Vergleiche mit einem Partner / einer Partnerin.**

What is it like?

13

Look at the pictures. Complete the sentences with adjectives from the box.
Sieh dir die Bilder an. Vervollständige die Sätze mit Adjektiven aus dem Kasten.

old · new · yummy · ~~lazy~~

Ava's ___lazy___ horse just stood there.

Tarek made some ________ milkshakes.

Lily moved into her ________ room.

Ellen went sightseeing in an ________ town.

My holiday post TARGET TASK

14 media worksheet E

Create a blog post about a holiday you dreamed about. Write down your ideas. You can add some photos or drawings.

Schreibe einen Blogpost über einen Urlaub, von dem du geträumt hast. Schreibe deine Ideen auf. Du kannst ein paar Fotos oder Zeichnungen hinzufügen.

My dream holiday

Where I went:

On my dream holiday I went

Who I went with:

I went with

Where I stayed:

What I did:

to Spain · to Poland · to Paris · to London · to the seaside · to the mountains · to a farm · ...

my family · my parents · my grandparents · my friend(s) · my brother · my sister · ...

at home · in a summer house · on a farm · in a hotel · on a houseboat · on a campsite · ...

visited ... · went to an adventure park · went hiking · took photos · looked at ... · played ... · cycled · listened to music · went swimming · had a picnic with ... · had a party with ... · ...

Sights of London

1a

Read the words and circle the London sights that you know.
Lies die Wörter und kreise die Londoner Sehenswürdigkeiten ein, die du kennst.

Buckingham Palace · the Tower of London · the River Thames ·
Tower Bridge · Hyde Park · Trafalgar Square · Big Ben · the London Eye ·
London Zoo · Wembley Stadium · ...

1b audio 6

Listen to the sounds and match them to the photos. Compare with a partner.
Höre dir die Geräusche an und ordne sie den Fotos zu. Vergleiche mit einem Partner / einer Partnerin.

Sound	1	2	3	4	5	6	7	8
Photo								

Tower Bridge A

View from the top of 20 Fenchurch Street B

Buckingham Palace C

The Natural History Museum D

The London Eye E

London Zoo F

Wembley Stadium G

Big Ben H

1c

Read the texts. Underline the name of the sight. In which photo on page 18 can you see the sight? Lies die Texte. Unterstreiche den Namen der Sehenswürdigkeit. Auf welchem Foto auf Seite 18 kann man die Sehenswürdigkeit sehen?

1 The London Eye is one of the tallest ferris wheels in Europe, and it is one of the most popular tourist attractions in the United Kingdom. When the weather is good, you can see all of London from the top.	Photo: E
2 Buckingham Palace is where the British king or queen lives and works. It is in the heart of London. There are 775 rooms.	Photo:
3 Big Ben is the name of the bell inside the Elizabeth Tower – a very tall clock tower at the Houses of Parliament near the River Thames. There is no lift inside the tower. You have to climb 334 stairs to get to the top.	Photo:
4 20 Fenchurch Street is a very tall skyscraper in London. You can get one of the best views of London from the café at the top.	Photo:
5 The Natural History Museum is a great place – and entry to the museum is free. The museum is most famous for its huge dinosaur exhibition. There are lots of skeletons, and you can even see a moving model of a T-Rex.	Photo:
6 London Zoo is one of the oldest zoos in the world. It opened in 1874. Today, you can see more than 19,000 animals and 673 different species there.	Photo:

1d

Which three sights do you like best? Write them down. Then talk to a partner. Welche drei Sehenswürdigkeiten magst du am liebsten? Schreibe sie auf. Sprich dann mit einem Partner / einer Partnerin.

1. ______________________

2. ______________________

3. ______________________

*My number **1** sight is …*

GRAMMAR HELP

Wenn du Personen oder Dinge näher beschreiben möchtest, verwendest du Adjektive (Wiewörter).
Möchtest du Personen oder Dinge vergleichen, kannst du Adjektive steigern.
Sieh dir die Beispiele an. Zähle die Silben der Adjektive. Was fällt dir auf?

Tower Bridge is **tall**,
Big Ben is **tall**er,
but the London Eye is **the tallest**.

I think Buckingham Palace is **famous**,
Tower Bridge is **more famous**,
but Big Ben is **the most famous**.

Die Adjektive **good** und **bad** haben unregelmäßige Formen:
good → better → the best   bad → worse → the worst

Different people

2

Look at the friends and complete the sentences with words from the box. **Sieh dir die Freunde an und vervollständige die Sätze mit Wörtern aus dem Kasten.**

longer than · the shortest · taller than · as tall as · shorter than

1 Noah is t__ __ __ __ __ __ __ __ __ __ Lily.
2 Lily's hair is l__ __ __ __ __ __ __ __ __ __ Harry's hair.
3 Ollie is s__ __ __ __ __ __ __ __ __ __ __ Tarek.
4 Ollie's legs are __ __ __ s__ __ __ __ __ __ __ .
5 Harry is __ __ __ __ __ __ __ __ Lily.

Good, better, the best

3

Fill in the missing forms. Look at the grammar box for help.
Trage die fehlenden Formen ein. Sieh dir zur Hilfe den Grammatikkasten an.

big	bigger	
short		
beautiful	more beautiful	
interesting		the most interesting
good		
bad		

Planning a day in London

4a

Look at the map. Talk about the sights. Take turns. Seht euch die Karte an. Sprecht über die Sehenswürdigkeiten. Wechselt einander ab.

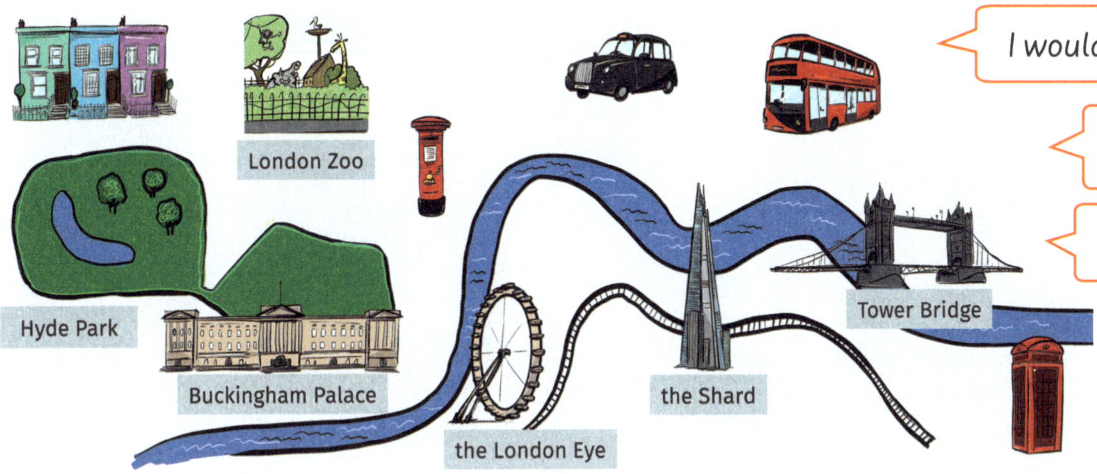

I would like to visit ...

I can see ...

... is near ...

4b

video 2, media worksheet A

Watch the video clip about London. Talk about it in German.
Seht euch den Videoclip über London an. Sprecht auf Deutsch darüber.

4c

audio 7

Ellen and her brother Nick from Brighton are visiting Harry and Lily. Listen to the children. Which of the sights in 4a are they talking about?
Ellen und ihr Bruder Nick aus Brighton besuchen Harry und Lily. Hört den Kindern zu. Über welche der Sehenswürdigkeiten aus 4a sprechen sie?

4d

audio 7

Listen again. Read and circle the right sentence endings.
Hört noch einmal zu. Lest und kreist die richtigen Satzenden ein.

1 Ellen would like to go to **the London Eye. / Buckingham Palace.**
2 Harry is interested in **London Zoo. / the Natural History Museum.**
3 Nick would like to see the sights **inside. / outside.**
4 Ellen thinks the London Eye is **more interesting. / more famous.**
5 The children think Lily's plan is **cool. / bad.**

Finding your way

6a

Look at the map of London. Point at the following streets and places.
Sieh dir die Karte von London an. Zeige auf die folgenden Straßen und Orte.

The River Thames | Westminster Bridge | Buckingham Palace | Spur Road | Queen Victoria Memorial | Birdcage Walk

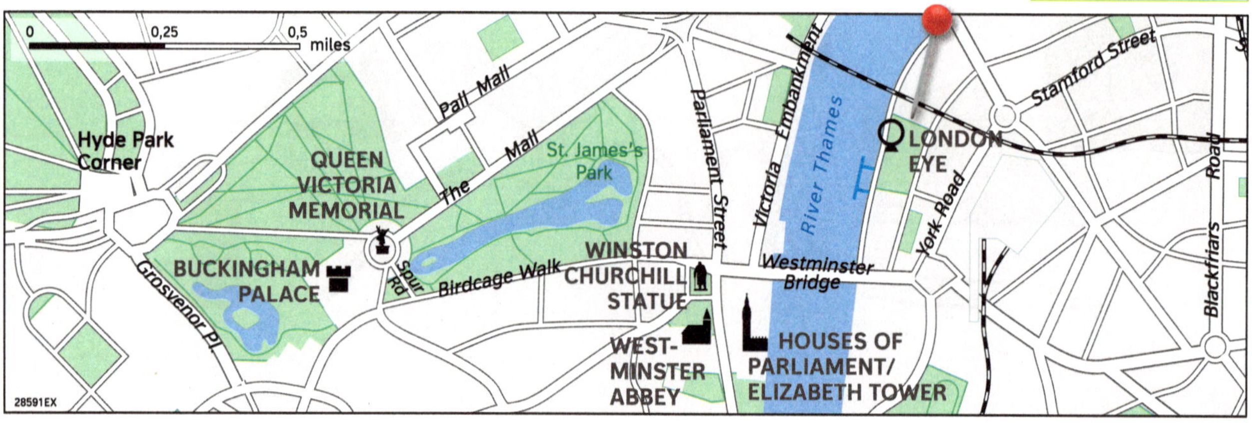

6b

audio 8

Listen to the dialogue and read the directions. Fill in where the family wants to go. Look at the map for help. Höre dir den Dialog an und lies die Wegbeschreibungen. Trage ein, wohin die Familie gehen will. Sieh dir die Karte an, wenn du Hilfe brauchst.

Just walk straight on ↑ along the river until you get to ↑ Westminster Bridge. Then turn right ↱ and cross ⇞ the river.
On your left you can see Big Ben. Then walk straight on ↑ until you get to Birdcage Walk. Then walk straight on – St. James's Park is on your right – turn right ↱ onto Spur Road.

Then you can see the Queen Victoria Memorial and ______________________.

6c

Give directions to a partner. Guide them through your classroom or your school. Take turns. Gib einem Partner / einer Partnerin Wegbeschreibungen. Leite ihn oder sie durch euer Klassenzimmer oder eure Schule. Wechselt einander ab.

↑	go straight on	↑	walk on until you get to ...
↰	turn left (onto)	⇤	on your left
↱	turn right (onto)	⇥	on your right
⇤ ⇥	walk past	⇞	cross the road / street / river

The London Eye

8a

Read Ellen's text message. What does she say about the view? Tick. ✓
Lies Ellens Sprachnachricht. Was sagt sie über die Aussicht? Mache ein Häkchen.

☐ The view is great. ☐ The view is interesting. ☐ The view is expensive.

Ellen Hi Mum, London is great! But it's really expensive. 😉 We're in a London Eye capsule right now. The view is very interesting. We can see the Tower of London and Tower Bridge – that's where we're going tomorrow. Talk to you later. Ellen and Nick xxx 12:43pm

8b

Write a text about another sight in London. **Schreibe eine Nachricht über eine andere Sehenswürdigkeit in London.**

Sieh auf Seite 19 nach, wenn du Hilfe brauchst. !

Hi ______________________________

London is ______________________________

Today I ______________________________

It ______________________________

____

____

Hier schreibst du, ...

... an wen du schreibst.

... wie du London findest.

... was du heute gemacht hast.

... wie das war.

... was du morgen machst.

... einen Gruß und deinen Namen.

LAND & LEUTE 1 video 3

Der *Tower of London*

Der Londoner Tower war unter anderem Wohnort früherer Könige und Königinnen, Zoo, Werkstatt, Lager, Waffenkammer, Museum und Gefängnis. Es gibt dort Wachleute, die eine sehr spezielle Uniform tragen. Zu ihren Pflichten gehört es, sich um die Raben im Tower zu kümmern.

Es leben dort immer mindestens sechs Raben. Einer Legende nach wird England untergehen, wenn die Raben den Tower verlassen.

Sieh dir das Video an. Was erfährst du noch über die Raben im Londoner Tower?

So much more to see and do

9a audio 9

It is breakfast time in Harry and Lily's house. Listen. Circle who is talking. Es ist Frühstückszeit bei Harry und Lily zu Hause. Höre zu. Kreise ein, wer spricht.

Ava · Mum · Harry · Tarek · Ellen · Lily · Nick

9b audio 9

Listen again. What are the children's plans for the afternoon? Tick. ✓ Höre noch einmal zu. Was sind die Pläne der Kinder für den Nachmittag? Mache Häkchen.

They want to do some shopping in ... ☐ Oxford Street. ☐ Covent Garden.

They want to see ... ☐ Platform 9¾. ☐ Platform 9.

9c

Read the texts. Which sights would you like to see? Talk about them in German. Take turns. Lies die Texte. Welche Sehenswürdigkeiten würdest du gerne sehen? Sprecht auf Deutsch über sie. Wechselt einander ab.

Covent Garden war früher ...

Bahnsteig 9¾ ist ...

Man kann dort ...

Heute ist Covent Garden berühmt für ...

Harry Potter-Fans wissen, dass von hier ...

Covent Garden Market was **a fruit and flower market** for hundreds of years. Today it is one of London's most popular shopping neighbourhoods with many outdoor cafés. You can **buy great clothes** there. Covent Garden is also **famous for street entertainment**. **Watch acrobats** or **listen to** one of the many **musicians**.

Platform 9¾ is a must for every Harry Potter fan. It is a train platform in King's Cross Station. It's not a real platform. It comes from the Harry Potter books. It looks like the entrance to the platform that students of Hogwarts use to get to their magical school.
Lots of people take photos with it. And the best thing about it is that it's free to visit!

9d

Read the questions and match the right answers.
Lies die Fragen und ordne die richtigen Antworten zu.

Es gibt mehr als eine Möglichkeit. !

1 What was Covent Garden for hundreds of years?

2 What is Covent Garden famous for today?

3 What can you do there?

- It was a fish market.
- You can see lots of skeletons.
- You can watch acrobats.
- You can meet Harry Potter there.
- It was a fruit and flower market.
- It is famous for street entertainment.
- You can listen to musicians.
- You can buy great clothes there.

Tower Bridge

10

A German family needs help understanding this flyer. Look at the flyer and answer their questions in German. Take turns.
Eine deutsche Familie braucht Hilfe dabei, den Flyer zu verstehen. Seht euch den Flyer an und beantwortet ihre Fragen auf Deutsch. Wechselt einander ab.

1 Worum geht es hier?

2 Was steht da über den Fußboden?

3 Wovor darf man keine Angst haben?

4 Wie viel kostet der Eintritt für Kinder?

5 Wie viel kostet der Eintritt für Erwachsene?

DON'T MISS THIS GREAT EXPERIENCE!

THE TOWER BRIDGE GLASS FLOOR WALKWAY

Did you know that you can walk on a glass floor high up inside Tower Bridge? Through the floor, you have a fantastic view of London below. The glass floor is 42 metres above the River Thames and 33.5 metres above the road. We hope you're not afraid of heights! Entry is £10.60 for adults and £5.30 for children. The Bridge is open every day from 9.30am to 6pm. Our address is Tower Bridge Road, London, SE1 2UP. The nearest Tube station is Tower Hill.

London

11

Make a word search with the names of some London sights.
Erstelle eine Wörtersuche mit den Namen einiger Londoner Sehenswürdigkeiten.

Auf S. 29 findest du ein Muster. !

Places

12a audio 10

Listen and repeat the names. **Höre zu und wiederhole die Namen.**

Tower Bridge · the London Eye · Big Ben · Buckingham Palace · London Zoo · the Natural History Museum · Wembley Stadium · the Houses of Parliament · Covent Garden · the Tower of London · Platform 9¾ · Madame Tussauds

12b

Match the sentence parts. **Ordne die Satzteile einander zu.**

1 Have a fantastic view	for children.
2 It is a perfect museum	is free.
3 London Zoo is one of	of the city!
4 Entry to the museum	the London Eye!
5 Don't miss the view from	the oldest zoos in the world.

Tourist attractions

13

Add the matching sentence parts. There are more parts than you need.
Füge die passenden Satzteile hinzu. Es gibt mehr Teile als du brauchst.

1 More than 19,000 animals ____________________.

2 There are lots of skeletons in the ____________________.

3 The London Eye is one of the most ____________________.

4 You have to climb 334 steps to get ____________________.

... to the top of the Elizabeth Tower.

... live in London Zoo.

... Natural History Museum.

... into Buckingham Palace.

... popular tourist attractions in London.

... live in Wembley Stadium.

A day out in London TARGET TASK

14 media worksheet C, D

Create one page for a travel guide for families in London.
Entwirf eine Seite für einen Reiseführer für Familien in London.

Step 1

Choose at least one London sight that is interesting for the whole family.
Wähle wenigstens eine Londoner Sehenswürdigkeit aus, die für die ganze Familie interessant ist.

Step 2

Collect information and pictures. You can use the Internet for your research.
Sammle Informationen und Bilder. Du kannst das Internet für deine Recherche nutzen.

Step 3

Make a draft of your page. Mache einen Entwurf deiner Seite.

Step 4

Ask a partner to look at your draft and edit it if necessary. Take turns.
Bitte einen Partner / eine Partnerin, sich deinen Entwurf anzusehen und bearbeite ihn, falls nötig. Wechselt einander ab.

Step 5

Create your page. Fill in the information and pictures.
Gestalte deine Seite. Trage die Informationen und Bilder ein.

Visit ...

What it is:

Your family day in London

You will never forget this famous sight!

What you can do there:

What people did in the holidays

Read the sentences and fill in the right verbs.
Lies die Sätze und trage die richtigen Verben ein.

~~went~~ · went hiking · went sightseeing · stayed · visited · had · played · took

1 The Brown family ___went___ to France.

2 My uncle ______ his friend in Paris.

3 Tom ______ at home and ______ a picnic with his friends.

4 My grandparents ______ me to an adventure park.

5 Sue and Jim ______ beach volleyball at the seaside.

6 James ______ in London.

7 Our neighbours ______ in the mountains.

True or false?

Did (+) or didn't (-) James do these things in London? Add the right answer. **Hat James diese Dinge in London gemacht oder nicht? Füge die richtige Antwort hinzu.**

Yes, he did. · No, he didn't.

Did James watch acrobats at Covent Garden? (+) ______

Did he visit the Natural History Museum? (-) ______

Did he see the famous Tower Bridge? (+) ______

Did he go to London Zoo? (-) ______

Do the word search

Find 12 adjectives. (8 → 4 ↓) Write them in the list on the left. Then add the matching forms from the box below. Finde 12 Adjektive. (8 → 4 ↓) Schreibe sie in die Liste links. Füge dann die passenden Formen aus dem Kasten unten hinzu.

x	o	l	d	w	s	l	o	n	g	r	t	f
t	a	l	l	a	h	k	l	c	b	n	m	a
s	g	h	z	y	o	u	n	g	u	i	p	m
m	i	n	t	e	r	e	s	t	i	n	g	o
a	g	f	a	n	t	a	s	t	i	c	b	u
l	f	w	g	o	o	d	l	o	p	i	a	s
l	e	x	p	e	n	s	i	v	e	s	d	f

old	older	the oldest
l		

~~older~~ · more fantastic · better · younger · the best · the longest · more famous · the most famous · more interesting · the most interesting · longer · the smallest · taller · shorter · the most fantastic · more expensive · the shortest · the most expensive · ~~the oldest~~ · worse · the tallest · the youngest · smaller · the worst

Important words

Sätze, um über deine Ferien zu sprechen:

In the holidays I ______

I often ______

One day ______

______

The weather was ______

______

______

Interessante Sehenswürdigkeiten in London und ihre Besonderheiten:

Buckingham Palace has ______

The London Eye is ______

______

______

______

Schöne Wörter zum Beschreiben von Personen und Dingen:

______

______

______

______

______

2

Celebrations

1 Look at the picture. What can you see?
2 What festivals or holidays do you celebrate?

Part A Festivals and traditions

- Du erfährst etwas über verschiedene Feste und Feiertage.
- Du sprichst über Neujahr und Halloween.
- Du gestaltest ein Poster zu einem Fest oder Feiertag.

Part B Let's celebrate!

- Du erfährst etwas über *Bonfire Night*.
- Du übst, über Pläne in der Zukunft zu sprechen.
- Du sammelst Ideen für ein Klassenfest und sprichst darüber.

Festivals

1a

Look at the words in the box and circle all the words for festivals and celebrations. Match them with the pictures.

Sieh dir die Wörter im Kasten an und kreise alle Wörter ein, die mit Festen zu tun haben. Ordne sie den Bildern zu.

school · Christmas · London · birthday · Monday · Halloween · breakfast

1b

Look at the photos and talk about them.

Seht euch die Fotos an und sprecht darüber.

3

5

2

- a boy and a man
- playing a game
- Hanukkah

- a happy family
- eating yummy food
- the end of Ramadan

- people
- Easter
- Easter egg roll

I can see a family.

I think they are celebrating Easter.

There is …

There are …

1c audio 11

Listen to the texts and read along. Match them with the photos.
Lies die Texte. Ordne sie den Fotos zu.

A	B	E

A Easter is a religious festival. Christians celebrate it in spring. In my family, we always have an Easter egg hunt on Easter Sunday. My little brother still believes in the Easter bunny.

B Eid is at the end of Ramadan. During Ramadan, Muslims only eat or drink after sunset. There are a lot of different traditions all over the world for Eid. In my family, we usually go to the mosque. In the evening we celebrate. There's always lots of food.

E Hanukkah is the Jewish festival of lights. For eight days in winter, people light a candle on a special candle holder called the Hanukkah menorah each night. In my family, we play games. In the picture, my father and me are playing with a dreidel. That's a typical Hanukkah game.

1d

Find the words in the text. **Finde die Wörter im Text.**

feiern = to c ______ Familie = f ______ Ostern = E ______

essen = to e ______ trinken = to d ______ Essen = f ______

Lichter = l ______ Kerze = c ______ Spiele = g ______

1e

Complete the sentences. **Vervollständige die Sätze.**

eat or drink after sunset. · all over the world for Eid. · Easter in spring. · religious festival. · Jewish festival of lights.

1 Easter is a ______.
2 Christians celebrate ______.
3 During Ramadan, Muslims only ______.
4 There are a lot of different traditions ______.
5 Hanukkah is the ______.

GRAMMAR HELP

Die Zeitform *simple present* kennst du schon. Du benutzt sie zum Beispiel,

- wenn jemand etwas regelmäßig tut oder
  wenn etwas regelmäßig stattfindet: Christians **celebrate** Easter in spring.
- oder wenn etwas über längere Zeit oder allgemein gültig ist: Eid **is** at the end of Ramadan.

Sieh dir die Beispielsätze an. Erinnerst du dich? Worauf musst du besonders achten?
This is Sam. He **celebrates** Hanukkah. He **doesn't celebrate** Eid.
Arta and Robert **celebrate** Eid. They **don't celebrate** Easter.

Christmas with my family

2

Circle the correct form of the verb and copy the sentences.
Kreise die richtige Form des Verbs ein und schreibe die Sätze ab.

1 We usually **doesn't** / **don't** celebrate Christmas at our house.

2 We **meet** / **meets** all our relatives at my granny's house in Hamburg.

3 Even my uncle and my aunt **come** / **comes** to Hamburg.

4 My granny always **gives** / **give** everyone lots of presents.

5 My father usually **get** / **gets** socks.

Celebrations

3

Underline the verbs in the first sentence. Then complete the second sentence with the nouns from the box. **Unterstreiche die Verben im ersten Satz. Vervollständige dann den zweiten Satz mit den Hauptwörtern aus dem Kasten.**

decorations · celebration · information · invitation

1 I invite my cousin to my party.
I send him an ___________.

2 My parents decorate the house.
The house is full of ___________.

3 My grandmother celebrates her birthday.
It's a big ___________.

4 Our teacher informs us about the class party.
She gives us a lot of ___________.

Happy New Year – all over the world

4a

audio 12

Look at the pictures and listen to the interviews.
Sieh dir die Bilder an und höre dir die Interviews an.

Reporter: My interview partner is Sharon. Sharon, you are from Scotland. Are there any special Scottish traditions?
Sharon: Well, we celebrate Hogmanay – that is the word for the last day of the year. We have the tradition of first footing. The first person who comes into the house after midnight brings good luck for the next year. He or she brings food or drink – sometimes salt, because salt stands for good luck!
Reporter: That sounds very interesting, thank you, Sharon!

Reporter: Paola, you are from Spain. Are there any special traditions for New Year's Eve in Spain?
Paola: When the bells ring at twelve o'clock, you have to eat one grape for each ring to welcome the new year. The grapes bring good luck for the next twelve months.
Reporter: Oh, I see. So it's really important to eat twelve grapes.

4b

Match the sentence parts. **Ordne die Satzteile einander zu.**

1 The Scottish word for	twelve grapes at midnight.
2 First footing means that the first	bring good luck for the new year.
3 People in Spain eat	New Year's Eve is "Hogmanay".
4 People in Spain believe that the grapes	guest in the new year brings good luck into the house.

What about you?

5

Talk about how you celebrate New Year with a partner.
Sprich mit einem Partner / einer Partnerin darüber, wie ihr Neujahr feiert.

have fireworks · dress up · celebrate · visit ... · dance · have good food · ...

Halloween

6a audio 13

Listen to the text and read along. Which words for food can you find?
Lies den Artikel. Welche Wörter für Essen kannst du finden?

Catholics from Ireland brought Halloween to the USA where it became a popular festival. The last evening in October, 31 October, was called "All Hallows' Eve". This is where the name Halloween comes from.

Irish people also brought the tradition of carving pumpkins into jack-o'-lanterns with them.

Today, Halloween is a very popular festival all over the world.

Many children like to dress up in scary costumes, have fun with apple bobbing and go trick-or-treating – although the sweets are probably more important to them than scaring away any ghosts.

6b

Read the text again. Write down the answers. Then do a quiz with a partner.
Lies den Artikel noch einmal. Schreibe die Antworten auf. Mache dann mit einem Partner / einer Partnerin ein Quiz.

1 Dieser Name kommt vom Namen All Hallows' Eve: H ______

2 Aus diesem Land haben die Menschen Halloween mitgebracht: I ______

3 Das sind geschnitzte und fantasievolle Kürbisse: j ______

4 Mit was verkleiden sich die Kinder gern an Halloween? s ______

5 Das machen Kinder gern an Halloween: go tr ______

6c

Read the text again. Write down five words from the text and add their German meaning. You can add words from another language that you know.

Lies den Text noch einmal. Schreibe fünf Wörter aus dem Text heraus und füge ihre deutsche Bedeutung hinzu. Du kannst Wörter aus einer anderen Sprache, die du kennst, ergänzen.

English	German	
festival		

LAND & LEUTE 2 video 4

Viele Kulturen – viele Feste

Im Vereinigten Königreich gibt es viele verschiedene Kulturen und Nationalitäten. Allein in London werden über 300 Sprachen gesprochen und es gibt viele unterschiedliche Kulturen und Religionen. Neben dem Christentum sind auch der Islam, der Buddhismus, der Hinduismus, das Judentum und der Sikhismus sehr verbreitet.

Durch diese Vielfalt gibt es über das Jahr verteilt viele verschiedene Feste, die nicht nur von den Anhängern einer Religion oder Kultur gefeiert werden, sondern von vielen Menschen in der Bevölkerung.

Manchmal fallen sogar Feste wie *Diwali* und *Bonfire Night*, auch *Guy Fawkes Night* genannt, auf das gleiche Datum und werden zusammen gefeiert.

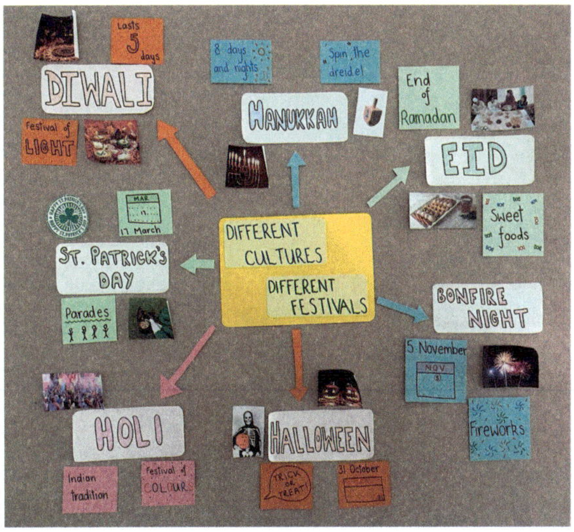

Welche Feste sind typisch für die Gegend, in der du wohnst?

Halloween today – opinions

7a

Read the statements about Halloween. Who likes Halloween? Who does not?
Lies die Aussagen über Halloween. Wer mag Halloween? Wer mag es nicht?

... likes ... | *... doesn't like ...*

I think Halloween is stupid! Dressing up in scary costumes is for little children.
I don't like going to people's houses and asking them for sweets! I don't like Halloween.

Tom, 13

I love Halloween! It's fun to dress up in scary costumes.
We go around the neighbourhood to collect sweets. You say: "Trick or treat".
My favourite costume is the mummy. You just have to wrap yourself in toilet paper and that's it!

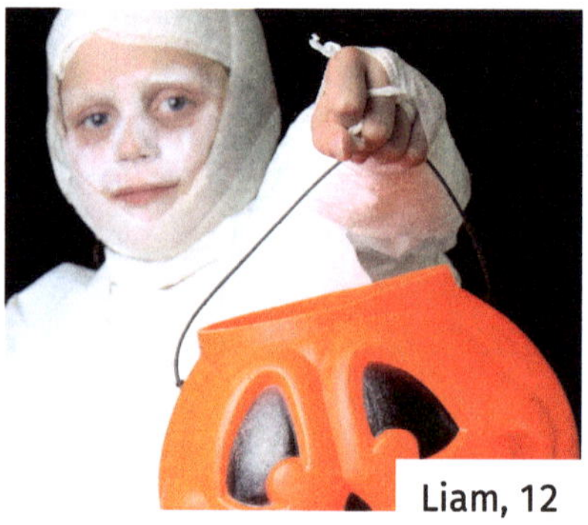
Liam, 12

7b

Read the statements about Halloween again. Find the English phrases and write them down. **Lies die Aussagen über Halloween noch einmal. Finde die englischen Ausdrücke und schreibe sie auf.**

Halloween ist blöd ____________________

Verkleiden ____________________

für kleine Kinder ____________________

um Süßigkeiten bitten ____________________

es macht Spaß ____________________

herumlaufen ____________________

Süßigkeiten sammeln ____________________

Lieblingskostüm ____________________

7c

Underline the statements about Halloween in the box. Use green for positive and red for negative statements.
Unterstreiche die Aussagen über Halloween im Kasten. Benutze grün für positive und rot für negative Aussagen.

It's fun to dress up in scary costumes. ·
Dressing up in scary costumes is for little children. ·
It's fun to go around the neighbourhood to collect sweets. ·
I don't like going to people's houses. ·
I love Halloween. · I think Halloween is stupid! ·
My favourite costume is the mummy.

7d

What do you think about Halloween? Write a short text.
Was hältst du von Halloween? Schreibe einen kurzen Text.

Hier schreibst du, ob du Halloween magst.
I love Halloween. / I like Halloween. / I don't like Halloween. / I think Halloween is stupid.

Hier schreibst du, ob du dich gern verkleidest.
It's fun to dress up. / Dressing up is for little children. / I like dressing up. / I don't like dressing up.

Hier schreibst du, ob du gern Süßigkeiten sammeln gehst.
Collecting sweets is fun. / Collecting sweets is stupid. / I like to go around the neighbourhood to collect sweets. / I don't like going to people's houses. / I like to ask people for sweets. / I don't like to ask people for sweets.

Halloween decorations

9

Read the text and explain in German how to make Halloween stress balls.
Lies den Text und erkläre auf Deutsch, wie man Halloween-Stressbälle macht.

Halloween stress balls

Don't worry, these stress balls are really easy to make. Use orange or white balloons to make pumpkin or ghost stress balls. Fill them with rice or sand. Take a felt-tip and draw a scary face on the balloons.

Celebrations during the year

10

Complete the sentences with phrases from the box.
Vervollständige die Sätze mit Ausdrücken aus dem Kasten.

first day of the new year. · winter and never in spring. · candle every evening. · end of Ramadan. · chocolate eggs.

1 At **Easter** people often give each other ______________________.

2 **Eid** is the celebration at the ______________________.

3 During **Hanukkah** people light a new ______________________.

4 **Christmas** is in ______________________.

5 **New Year's Day** is the ______________________.

Categories

11a

Read the words in the box. Sort them into the table.
Lies die Wörter im Kasten. Sortiere sie in die Tabelle.

candles · eggs · Eid · Jewish · food · Ramadan · mosque · Muslim · Easter · menorah · Christian · Hanukkah

religion	festival	other words

11b

Add more words if you like. **Füge weitere Wörter hinzu, wenn du möchtest.**

A festival poster TARGET TASK

12

Your task is to present a festival or a holiday on a poster.
Deine Aufgabe ist es, ein Fest oder einen Feiertag auf einem Poster zu präsentieren.

My festival: ______________________ (**Wie** heißt das Fest?)

Who? ______________________ (**Wer** feiert das Fest?)

When? ______________________ (**Wann** wird es gefeiert?)

Where? ______________________ (**Wo** wird gefeiert?)

What? ______________________ (**Was** machen die Menschen?)

What? ______________________ (**Was** essen sie?)

Five festival words

____

____

____

____

____

A picture of the festival

A Bonfire Night flyer

1a

Look at the photo of a bonfire. Do you know any festivals with bonfires? Talk about them with a partner.
Sieh dir das Foto eines Freudenfeuers an. Kennst du Feste mit Freudenfeuern? Sprich mit einem Partner / einer Partnerin darüber.

1b

Look at the flyer. What is it about? **Sieh dir den Flyer an. Worum geht es?**

1c

Look at the flyer again. Number the sentences.
Sieh dir den Flyer noch einmal an. Nummeriere die Sätze.

- [ ] Hier steht, dass es ein tolles Feuerwerk gibt.
- [ ] Hier steht der Name der Party.
- [ ] Hier kann man sehen, an welchem Tag das Fest ist.
- [ ] Hier steht, wieviel der Eintritt kostet.
- 1 Hier kann man sehen, dass es auch Livemusik gibt.

Bonfire Night plans

2a

audio 14

Listen to Lily, Harry and their mums and read along. What are they talking about? **Hört Lily, Harry und ihren Müttern zu und lest mit. Worüber sprechen sie?**

Lily: It's Bonfire Night on Saturday. The fireworks in Brighton were always so cool! So what are we doing this year?
Harry: I found this flyer in a shop yesterday. There is a big party here in Notting Hill. It looks cool. They are having live music, a funfair and food stalls – just like in Brighton.
Lily: That sounds great.
Sarah: Can I look at the flyer, please? Hmm, it's expensive. It costs five pounds for kids and even more for adults. I'm not paying that much money to stand out in the cold.
Olivia: And I don't like big parties. Usually they're full of people and it's so loud.
Sarah: Phew, I also don't think that the party is a good idea. What are your friends doing for Bonfire Night?
Harry: Tarek and his dad are going to the big firework show at Alexandra Palace again. Last year it was really good. Maybe we can go with them?
Lily: Let's talk to Ava and Tarek tomorrow. But I really want to celebrate Bonfire Night because ...
Harry: ... you can eat lots of toffee apples.
Lily: Yeah! Toffee apples are the best thing about Bonfire Night.

2b

Read the dialogue again and match the sentence parts. Write down the sentences. **Lies den Dialog noch einmal und ordne die Satzteile einander zu. Schreibe die Sätze auf.**

1 Lily says that the fireworks	to stand out in the cold.
2 Harry found a flyer for	in Brighton were always so cool.
3 Sarah is not paying that much money	going to Alexandra Palace.
4 Tarek and his dad are	a big Bonfire Night party in Notting Hill.

GRAMMAR HELP

Die Zeitform *present progressive* kennst du bereits. Du benutzt es, um auszudrücken, was jemand gerade macht. Du kannst es aber auch benutzen, um etwas über die nahe Zukunft zu sagen.

Wenn du über **einen** Menschen sprichst, benutzt du ***is*** und hängst ***-ing*** ans Verb:
She **is watching** the fireworks next weekend. He **is having** a party next Saturday.
She **is not (= isn't) working** in the garden tomorrow.

Wenn du über **mehrere** Menschen sprichst, benutzt du ***are*** und hängst ***-ing*** ans Verb:
We **are watching** the fireworks next weekend. We **are having** a party next Saturday.
We **are not (= aren't) working** in the garden tomorrow.

What is Tarek planning for next week?

3

Complete the sentences. Vervollständige die Sätze.

Next Monday afternoon Tarek *is playing* ______ (play) hockey.

Next Tuesday Tarek ______ (watch) a football match with his dad.

Next Wednesday Tarek *is not* ______ (meet) Uncle Sami.

Next Thursday Tarek ______ (do) science experiments at the school lab.

Next Friday afternoon Tarek ______ (go) to the cinema.

Sound check

5a audio 15

Listen to the words and repeat them. Höre dir die Wörter an und wiederhole sie.

celebrate · remember · expensive · yesterday · fireworks · chocolate · fantastic · November

5b

Where is the stress? Make two lists. Wo ist die Betonung? Mache zwei Listen.

stress on the first syllable	stress on the second syllable
celebrate, ______	*remember,* ______
______	______

5c audio 16

Listen and check your lists. Höre zu und überprüfe deine Listen.

A special Bonfire Night

6a

audio 17

Listen and read along. What is the friends' plan? Höre zu und lies mit. Was ist der Plan der Freunde?

Lily: Bonfire Night is almost here. So, what are your plans for Saturday?
Harry: Maybe we could have our own Bonfire Night Party? We could ask our mums if we can do it at our place. Everybody brings something to eat or to drink, and we can play games like apple bobbing ...
Lily: Haha Harry, isn't that for children ...? But ... it could be fun, too. Our own party ... sounds good to me!
Ava: Brilliant idea! Let's do it! I can make toffee apples. How many do we need?
Lily: Lots! I love toffee apples. Any more ideas?
Tarek: I can bring hot apple juice and hot chocolate. How much wood do we need for the fire?
Ava: Noah and I can bring the wood. I'm sure our dad can help us. Let me just text him.
Harry: Why don't we cook some jacket potatoes in the fire?
Lily: Oh man, it's going to be the best Bonfire Night party ever! Let's make a list.

6b

Ava is writing a text message to her dad. Fill in the gaps with the words from the box. Ava scheibt ihrem Vater eine Nachricht. Fülle die Lücken mit Wörtern aus dem Kasten aus.

bring · Bonfire Night · drink · wood · talking · place

Hi Dad. I'm with Harry, Lily and Noah and we're t _ _ _ _ _ _

about our plans for B _ _ _ _ _ _ _ _ _ _ _.

We'd love to have our own party at Harry and Lily's p _ _ _ _ this year.

We would all b _ _ _ _ something to eat and to d _ _ _ _.

But we need your help with the w _ _ _ for the fire. Could you do that?

Please?

A Bonfire Night recipe

7a

Look at the pictures and match them with the words.
Sieh dir die Bilder an und ordne sie den Wörtern zu.

bowl   skewer   sugar   apple

7b

Look at the recipe. What is it for? **Sieh dir das Rezept an. Für was ist es?**

☐ sugar apples   ☐ chocolate apples   ☐ toffee apples

You need: 8 apples, 400 g sugar, 1 tablespoon lemon juice, 100 ml water

Step 1
Place the apples in a large bowl, then cover with boiling water. Dry the apples.

Step 2
Push a wooden skewer into each apple.

Step 3
Put the apples on a sheet of baking paper. Put the sugar and the water into a pot. Cook for 5 minutes until the sugar melts, then add the lemon juice.

Step 4
Put each apple in the pot with the hot toffee, then place on the baking paper. Leave the toffee to cool: Enjoy!

7b

Read the recipe again and look at the pictures. Write these steps in the right order. **Lies das Rezept noch einmal und sieh dir die Bilder an. Schreibe diese Schritte in der richtigen Reihenfolge auf.**

Put each apple in the pot with the hot toffee. · Wash and dry the apples. · Let the toffee apples cool before you eat them. · Put wooden skewers into the apples.

Bonfire Night safety tips

8a

video 5, media worksheet A

Watch the video clip. Then match the words with the sentences.
Sieh dir den Videoclip an. Ordne dann die Wörter den Sätzen zu.

CHECK	throw fireworks at people or animals.
BE	that there are no animals in your bonfire.
NEVER	careful when you use sparklers.

8b

Draw some fireworks and colour them in different colours. Name the colours.
Zeichne Feuerwerk und male es in verschiedenen Farben aus. Benenne die Farben.

My colours: ______ = ______, ______ = ______,
______ = ______, ______ = ______

LAND & LEUTE 3 video 6

Bonfire Night

Am 5. November feiern die Menschen in Großbritannien *Bonfire Night* oder *Guy Fawkes Night* mit großen Freudenfeuern *(bonfires)* und Feuerwerk *(fireworks)*.

Der Grund: Im Jahr 1605 hatte sich eine Gruppe von Männern, unter ihnen Guy Fawkes, gegen den König verschworen. Sie wollten ihn und die Mitglieder des Parlaments durch eine Explosion mit Schießpulver töten. Dieses Ereignis nennt man die Pulververschwörung *(the Gunpowder Plot)*. Die Männer wurden aber entdeckt und gefangen genommen. Der König und die Mitglieder des Parlaments blieben unverletzt und das feiert man seitdem an diesem Tag.

Lange gehörte das Herstellen einer Art Strohpuppe, die Guy Fawkes darstellen sollte, dazu: Kinder bastelten eine solche Puppe und sammelten Geld. Diese Puppe wurde dann mit verbrannt. Heute machen das nur noch wenige Menschen.

Mittlerweile verzichten viele Menschen auf privates Feuerwerk, achten darauf, dass sie nichts verbrennen, das schädliche Gase produziert und versuchen, möglichst wenig Abfall zu produzieren.

Welche Feiertage, die auf ein geschichtliches Ereignis zurückgehen, kennst du noch?

Asking Mum

9a audio 18

Listen to Harry and his mum and read along.
Höre Harry und seiner Mutter zu und lies mit.

Harry: Hi Mum.
Sarah: Hi Harry. What's this about a Bonfire Night party at our place?
Harry: We want to organize our own Bonfire Night Party ...
Sarah: Oh, dear. I don't want to have all the work this weekend! Really ...
Harry: Don't worry about the work. We already made a plan! Ava and Noah are bringing wood and Ava is making toffee apples, and Tarek is ...
Sarah: OK, I see ... Maybe it's not such a bad idea.
Harry: Oh, thank you so much, Mum! You are the best! ... Noah and Tarek are crazy about fireworks. So, can we buy some? Bonfire Night is no fun without fireworks.
Sarah: I'm not spending lots of money on fireworks. It's so expensive! And really bad for the environment. And the animals are scared of the noise.
Harry: Well ... what are we going to do then?
Sarah: I read that Alexandra Palace is streaming their fireworks display via its website. So we can watch their fireworks display in our living room.
Harry: I guess we could do that ...

9b audio 18

Listen again. Circle the right words.
Höre noch einmal zu. Kreise die richtigen Wörter ein.

1 Sarah thinks that fireworks are **expensive / beautiful**.

2 Animals are often scared of the **apples / noise**.

3 Sarah thinks they can watch the fireworks display in **the garden / the living room**.

Remember, remember ...

10 audio 19

There is an old rhyme about the Gunpowder Plot. Listen to the rhyme and read along aloud.
Es gibt einen alten Reim über die Pulverschwörung. Hört euch den Reim an und lest laut mit.

Remember, remember
The fifth of November,
Gunpowder, treason and plot.
I see no reason
Why gunpowder treason
Should ever be forgot.

The Bonfire Night party

12a

Read Ava's text message. Underline the words that tell you how the party is.
Lies Avas Textnachricht. Unterstreiche die Wörter, die dir sagen, wie die Party ist.

Ava Hi Mum, we are having a good time. Noah and Tarek are roasting marshmallows on the bonfire. Earlier we grilled sausages and cooked jacket potatoes in the fire. So good! Lily is eating one of my toffee apples, they are really yummy. Later we are watching the fireworks live stream from Alexandra Palace and lighting more sparklers. See u. Love, Ava Saturday 9:17pm

12b

Look at the picture and describe it.
Sieh dir das Bild an und beschreibe es.

house · table · food · garden · fire · ...

I can see ...

On the left there is ...

In the background there is ...

12c

What is everyone doing? Was macht jeder?

is writing ... · are roasting ... · is eating ... · are watching ... · are talking ... · ...

Ava is writing a text. Lily ...

Harry ...

Noah and Tarek ...

Olivia and Sarah ...

Talking about ideas

14

Match the sentence parts. Write down the sentences.
Verbinde die Satzteile. Schreibe die Sätze auf.

1 Have you got any	some biscuits.
2 We should dress up	with a few pumpkins.
3 We could decorate the room	ideas for cool games?
4 I think we need	different countries?
5 What about food from	in scary costumes.

____

____

____

____

____

A party checklist

15

Tarek is planning a party at his house. Complete the sentences with *some* or *any*.
Tarek plant eine Party zu Hause. Vervollständige die Sätze mit *some* oder *any*.

some verwendest du in gewöhnlichen Aussagesätzen:
any verwendest du in Fragen und verneinten Sätzen:

We need **some** apples.
Do we need **any** bananas?
We don't need **any** oranges.

First of all I need ______________ cool music. Do I have ______________ good music for dancing? I need to check that. I should get ______________ fun games, too. And I need ______________ balloons to decorate the room. I need ______________ sweets and crisps. But I should get ______________ healthy snacks and something to drink, too. We haven't got ______________ orange juice.

Our class party TARGET TASK

16a

Your task is to make plans for a class party. Fill in the checklist first.
Deine Aufgabe ist es, Pläne für eine Klassenparty zu machen. Fülle zuerst die Checkliste aus.

What kind of party is it? A ______________________ party
(Halloween, Christmas, Bonfire Night, carnival, pool, Mexican, Turkish, ...)

When is the party? ______________________
(Monday, Tuesday, ..., 10am, 1 pm, 11th November, ...)

Where is the party? ______________________
(in the classroom, on the football field, ...)

What is interesting about the party? ______________________
(food, drinks, firework, dancing, theatre, ...)

How much do children have to pay for food and drink? ______________________

16b

Now create your poster. Fill in the words and colour it.
Entwirf nun dein Poster. Trage die Wörter ein und male es bunt.

Come to our ______________________ party!

When? ______________________

Where? ______________________

Food and drink:

____

____

Activities:

____

____

Prices for food and drink:

____

____

What do they like?

1

Dean likes apples.
He doesn't like pumpkins.

Tammy ________________________________.

She ________________________________.

The children like sweets.
They don't like bananas.

They ________________________________.

They ________________________________.

What is it about?

2a

The two texts are mixed up. Which one is about Halloween, which one is about Easter? Colour the sentences.

Die zwei Texte sind durcheinander geraten. Welcher ist über Halloween, welcher ist über Ostern? Male die Sätze farbig an.

Easter is a religious festival. Halloween is in autumn. It's fun to dress up in scary costumes. We go around the neighbourhood to collect sweets. Christians celebrate it in spring. You say: "Trick or treat". In my family, we always have an Easter egg hunt on Easter Sunday. My favourite costume is the mummy. My little brother still believes in the Easter bunny.

2b

Copy the texts in the right order in your exercise book.

Schreibe die Texte in der richtigen Reihenfolge in deinem Heft ab.

Easter: Easter is a religious festival. Christians ...

Halloween:

Plans for next Saturday

3

Look at the family planner. Say what the people are doing or not doing. **Sieh dir den Familienplanner an. Sage, was die Menschen machen oder nicht machen.**

Saturday

Mum	help Sam with her homework	clean the living room	~~buy food~~
Grandma and Grandpa	~~read a book~~	go for a walk	cook a delicious dinner

On Saturday, Mum **is helping** Sam with her homework.

On Saturday, Grandma and Grandpa **aren't reading** a book.

The party table

4

Are the words on the table party words? Sort them into the right lists.
Sind die Wörter auf dem Tisch Partywörter? Sortiere sie in die richtigen Listen.

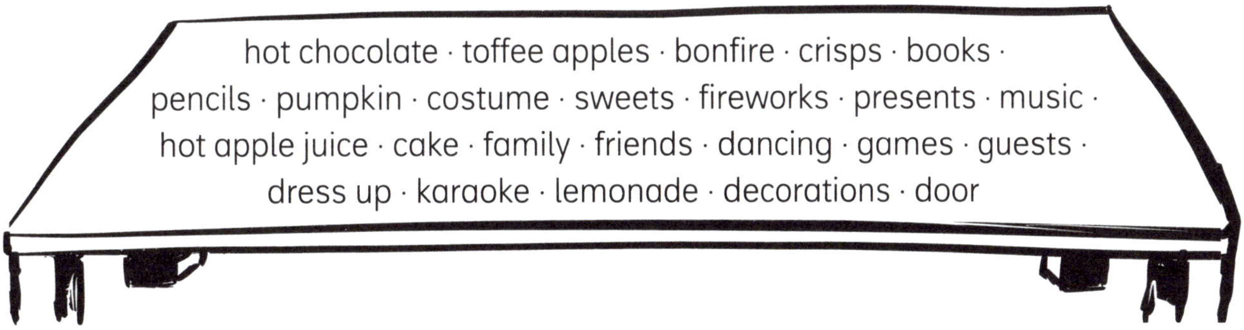

Party words

Other words

Important words

Festival words:

So kann ich über die nahe Zukunft sprechen:

I am playing football on Saturday.

...

Diese Wörter mag ich besonders gern:

3

Living together

1 What can you see in the picture?
2 What do you think is the problem? Collect ideas.

Part A Getting along

- Du sprichst über Regeln.
- Du erfährst etwas über Schulregeln an einer britischen Schule.
- Du präsentierst ein Rollenspiel über die Lösung eines Konflikts.

Part B Take care!

- Du sprichst über Ausflüge in die Natur.
- Du erfährst etwas über die Tierwelt Großbritanniens.
- Du entwickelst eine Idee für ein Umweltprojekt.

School rules

1a

Talk about the rules at your school. Look at the examples.
Sprecht über die Regeln an eurer Schule. Seht euch die Beispiele an.

We can't drink during lessons.

drink during lessons

eat in the classroom

run in the school building

be late

use a mobile phone at school

1b

Read the Holland Park School rules. **Lies die Regeln der Holland Park School.**

SCHOOL RULES

☐ 1. Be polite and show respect for other students and the teachers.

☐ 2. School starts at 8:40am. Students who are late must first report to the headteacher's office.

☐ 3. Students must not run in the school building.

☐ 4. Students must wear the correct school uniform.

☐ 5. Eating is not allowed in the classrooms.

☐ 6. Students are not allowed to wear make-up or piercings.

☐ 7. Students are not allowed to wear hats or caps on school grounds.

☐ 8. Students are not allowed to use mobile phones at school.

1c

Find the words in the text. Finde die Wörter im Text.

höflich	p ______	Respekt zeigen	show r ______
sich anmelden	r ______	Schulleiter	h ______
erlaubt	a ______	Schulgelände	school g ______

1d

Tick ✓ the rules in 1b that are the same at your school. What is different? Talk about the rules. Mache ein Häkchen an die Regeln in 1b, die an deiner Schule gleich sind. Was ist anders? Sprecht über die Regeln.

At our school we also have rule number …

Rule number … is different at our school.

1e

Look at the pictures. Which rules are the students breaking? Complete the sentences. Sieh dir die Bilder an. Welche Regeln brechen die Schülerinnen und Schüler? Vervollständige die Sätze.

The girl in picture one is breaking rule number ____.

Students must wear the ______

The boy in picture two is breaking rule number ____.

Students have to be ______

The boy in picture three is breaking rule number ____.

Students must not ______

The girl in picture four is breaking rule number ____.

Students are not allowed ______

Your opinion

2

Which of the rules do you find important or not important? Talk about them. Welche der Regeln findet ihr wichtig oder nicht wichtig? Sprecht über sie.

GRAMMAR HELP

Wenn du über Regeln sprechen willst, kannst du die Wörter **must** und **mustn't** benutzen. Schau dir die Beispiele an.

Harry **must** wear the correct school uniform.	Harry **muss** die richtige Schuluniform tragen.
We **must** always be on time.	Wir **müssen** immer pünktlich sein.
Ava **mustn't** listen to music when she does her homework.	Ava **darf nicht** Musik hören, wenn sie ihre Hausaufgaben macht.
Students **mustn't** talk during tests.	Die Schülerinnen und Schüler **dürfen** während Tests **nicht** sprechen.

Rules

3

Read the school rules and complete the sentences with must (+) or mustn't (–).

Lies die Schulregeln und vervollständige die Sätze mit *must* oder *mustn't*.

1 You ___mustn't___ sleep in class. (–)

2 You ______________ arrive late to school. (–)

3 You ______________ bring your books to school every day. (+)

4 You ______________ play football in class. (–)

5 You ______________ listen to your teacher. (+)

Rules at our school

4

Match the sentence parts and write down the rules.

Ordne die Satzteile einander zu und schreibe die Regeln auf.

1 We can bring our mobile phones to school, but we	mustn't eat in the classroom.
2 We can bring our own lunch, but we	mustn't ride them on the school grounds.
3 We are allowed to wear cool clothes, but we	mustn't use them during lessons.
4 We are allowed to ride our bikes to school, but we	must take off caps during lessons.

Dress code

6a

Look at the picture. Then number the words.

Sieh dir das Bild an. Nummeriere dann die Wörter.

☐ shirt

☐ blazer

☐ tie

☐ trousers

☐ shoes

☐ skirt

6b audio 20

Listen to Ava, Tarek and Lily. What are they talking about? Tick. ✓

Höre Ava, Tarek und Lily zu. Worüber sprechen sie? Mache ein Häkchen.

☐ school dinner ☐ new teachers ☐ school rules

6c audio 20

Listen again. Circle the correct words. Then write down the sentences.

Höre noch einmal zu. Kreise die richtigen Wörter ein. Schreibe dann die Sätze auf.

1 Lily is in trouble because her **skirt was / trousers were** too short.

2 Usually Tarek doesn't get into trouble because he always wears the correct school uniform **at home / at school**.

3 Ava doesn't like the dress code because she wants to **express her style / wear a red blazer**.

4 Tarek was in trouble last week because he **ran in the school building / was late**.

LAND & LEUTE 4 video 7

Schuluniformen

In Großbritannien tragen die Schülerinnen und Schüler an fast allen Schulen Schuluniformen. Es gibt allerdings Ausnahmen. An einigen Schulen darf man am Freitag etwas lässiger gekleidet sein. Auch für Wohltätigkeitsprojekte gibt es solche Ausnahmen.

Sieh dir das Video an. Findest du Schuluniformen gut?

Talking about problems

7a

Look at the pictures and read the sentences. Which one goes with which picture? Talk about them with a partner. Sieh dir die Bilder an und lies die Sätze. Welcher passt zu welchem Bild? Sprich mit einem Partner / einer Partnerin darüber.

Harry and Lily look annoyed. ☐

Tarek's dad looks annoyed. ☐

Mum and Dad look angry and worried. ☐

Picture A goes with …

7b audio 21

Listen to the dialogues. Which one goes with which picture?
Höre dir die Dialoge an. Welcher passt zu welchem Bild?

Dialogue 1	Dialogue 2	Dialogue 3
Picture ☐	Picture ☐	Picture ☐

7c

Think about the people's feelings. Fill in the names. Compare with a partner.
Denke über die Gefühle der Menschen nach. Trage die Namen ein. Vergleicht.

______ feels angry. ______ feel annoyed.

______ feels happy. ______ feel worried.

______ feel relaxed. ______ feels tired.

Family problems

8a

Look at the picture. What do you think Dad and Joshua are saying? Circle. Compare with a partner. Sieh dir das Bild an. Was sagen Papa und Joshua wohl? Kreise ein. Vergleiche mit einem Partner / einer Partnerin.

It's too late!

I want to watch the film!

Are you hungry?

Go to bed!

I'm worried!

Only five more minutes!

You look very tired!

Let's go swimming!

Stop playing games!

There's a quiz show on TV.

There's a football match on TV.

Stop watching TV!

8b

Read what Dad and Joshua are saying and colour the sentences: what Dad says in red, what Joshua says in yellow. Lies, was Papa und Joshua sagen und male die Sätze an: Was Papa sagt in rot, was Joshua sagt in gelb.

Oh no! What's going on here?

Sssshh. It's exciting, Dad.

Look, the monsters are attacking the man.

Stop watching TV at this time! It's too late.

But I'm not tired!

No? Then look at yourself! You look very tired!

Only five more minutes. Please!

School is starting late tomorrow.

No discussion! Switch off the TV and go to bed.

Ava's diary

10a

Read Ava's diary entry. How does she feel? Tick. ✓
Lies Avas Tagebucheintrag. Wie fühlt sie sich? Mache ein Häkchen.

☐ happy ☐ angry ☐ tired

Wednesday 7th February

Why can't I do what I want? Mum always knows better.

I've got some cool new jeans, but Mum says I'm not allowed to wear them to Dad's birthday party. And I'm not allowed to wear make-up.

Everybody else can use their phone until ten. I can't. Mum says I must be in bed by half past nine. ***Rules, rules, rules!*** *That's all we have in this house!* ***I hate them!!!***

And I always have to be home by seven. Then there is school! I'm not allowed to listen to music or check my phone when I do my homework. And I have to finish it before I can go out or play with Ollie.

On Saturday we are having a family meeting to discuss when Noah and I have to be at home at the weekend. I hope Dad is on our side. Sometimes he's not as strict as Mum.

10b

Read the German sentences. Tick ✓ true or false.
Lies die deutschen Sätze. Mache ein Häkchen bei richtig oder falsch.

	true	false
Ava soll zu Papas Geburtstagsparty die neue Jeans anziehen.		
Sie darf kein Make-up tragen.		
Ava muss bis halb zwölf im Bett sein.		
Ava muss bis acht Uhr zu Hause sein.		
Während der Hausaufgaben darf Ava klassische Musik hören.		
Am Samstag hat Avas Familie eine Familienkonferenz.		

The family meeting

11a

What do you think: what do Ava and Noah want? Tick. ✓
Was wollen Ava und Noah wohl? Mache ein Häkchen.

☐ They want to get more pocket money. ☐ They want to stay out longer.

11b

audio 22

Listen to the dialogue and read along. Do Ava and Noah get what they want?
Höre dir den Dialog an und lies mit. Bekommen Ava und Noah, was sie wollen?

Dad: OK everyone, welcome to today's family meeting. Our first point is: when do Ava and Noah have to be home at the weekends?
Ava: Seven o'clock for me and eight o'clock for Noah is much too early. All my friends are allowed to stay out until eight. That's not fair!
Noah: And Tim is allowed to stay out until nine on Friday and Saturday!
Mum: Don't interrupt your sister, please.
Ava: But he's right. Why do we have to be home so early? We're not babies anymore.
Mum: Your dad and I think that you're still too young to stay out so late. And last Saturday Noah was so late that I don't think we should change the rules.
Ava: I was always on time!
Noah: What about trying something: Ava and I come home on time and stick to all our family rules for two weeks. If that works, I can stay out until nine and Ava until eight on Fridays and Saturdays.
Ava: Yes, please! I think that's a good idea.
Mum: Well, OK. I think I can live with that.

11c

Who says what? Write it down and compare with a partner.
Wer sagt was? Schreibe es auf und vergleicht zu zweit.

1 Wann sollen Ava und Noah an den Wochenenden zu Hause sein? Dad
2 Tim darf freitags und samstags bis 9 Uhr wegbleiben. ______
3 Wir sind doch keine Babys mehr! ______
4 Ihr seid noch zu jung, um so spät wegzubleiben. ______
5 Wenn das klappt, darf ich freitags und samstags bis neun und Ava bis acht Uhr wegbleiben. ______
6 Ich glaube, damit kann ich leben. ______

Dad, can I …?

13a

Match Dad's answers to the boy's questions. Number them.
Ordne Papas Antworten den Fragen des Jungen zu. Nummeriere sie.

Dad, can I …

1 ... watch TV after ten?

2 ... do my homework later?

3 ... wear my cool new jeans?

4 ... meet some friends at the park?

Yes, but …

... not today. You can meet them on Saturday. ____

... not for Grandma's birthday. ____

... not a horror film. ____

... do it before you go out. ____

13b

Practise the dialogue with a partner. **Übt den Dialog zu zweit.**

Asking questions

14

Unscramble the questions and the answers. Then write them down.
Entwirre die Fragen und die Antworten. Schreibe sie dann auf.

1 at home? – have to be – When do we | o'clock. – At nine

____

2 to watch – Are you allowed – TV until 10pm? | I'm not. – No,

____

3 play – computer games? – Can I | you can't. – No,

____

4 Why – wear make-up? – can't I | too young. – that you are – We think

____

A family meeting TARGET TASK

15 media worksheet B, F

Do a role play of a family meeting. Mache ein Rollenspiel einer Familienkonferenz.

Step 1

Work in small groups. Arbeitet in Kleingruppen.

Step 2

Plan your role play. Plant euer Rollenspiel.

- The reason for the meeting is: The children want their own smartphones.
- These family members take part in the meeting:

____

- What could be a solution?
  use an old phone / buy a second-hand phone / wait until Christmas / ask the grandparents / ...

Step 3

What could the family members say? Collect ideas.
Was könnten die Familienmitglieder sagen? Sammle Ideen.

Child: *I want my own smartphone. All the children at school have got one. When I have a problem I can call you or send a message.*

Dad: *Smartphones are very expensive! You are too young!*

Mum: *Couldn't we look for second-hand phones? They are cheaper.*

Other Ideas: *We could ...* ______________________________

____

Step 4

Decide who is playing which role. Entscheidet, wer welche Rolle spielt.

Child: ______________ Dad: ______________

Mum: ______________

Step 5

Practise your role play and then present it. You can make a recording or a video clip.
Übt euer Rollenspiel und stellt es dann vor. Ihr könnt eine Aufnahme oder einen Videoclip machen.

Tips for a great day out

1a

Look at the flyers. What can you see? Circle the matching words in the box.
Sieh dir die Flyer an. Was kannst du sehen? Kreise die passenden Wörter im Kasten ein.

panda · beach · forest · fox · lion · deer · sand · people · helicopter · sea

BRITISH WILDLIFE CENTRE

Discover Britain's wildlife!

Discover British wildlife at the British Wildlife Centre all year round!

From foxes, deer and red squirrels to fish and birds there is a whole world of wildlife waiting for you just 25 miles away from London!

Go to our website before your visit. There you can find a map, animal feeding times, and much more information.

Please note:

- You can book tickets online.
- Do not feed the animals.
- Parking is free.
- Open from 10am every day. Closed 25 December.

Welcome to Southwold Beach!

THE place for family fun

Please help us to keep the beach safe and beautiful. Here are our beach rules:

- Swim between the blue flags.
- Parents must watch their children in the water at all times.
- Take your rubbish with you when you leave.
- Respect other beach visitors.
- No fires or barbecues.
- No dogs on the beach from May to October.
- No glass bottles on the beach.
- No loud music.

Please make sure that you use enough sun cream!

1b

Read the flyers. Which place would you go to? Why? You can look at the box for help. **Lies die Flyer. Welchen Ort würdest du besuchen? Warum? Du kannst dir den Kasten ansehen, wenn du Hilfe brauchst.**

It is open all year round. · There is a beach. · You do not need tickets. · You can swim there. · It is near London. · Parking is free. · There is no loud music. · You can book tickets online. · You can see many animals.

I think ____________________ *is the most interesting*

because ____________________

1c

Are the statements true or false? Tick. ✓
Sind die Aussagen richtig oder falsch? Mache ein Häkchen.

		true	false
1	You can see foxes at the Wildlife Centre.		
2	The Wildlife Centre has not got a website.		
3	You are allowed to feed the animals.		
4	You have to pay for parking at the Wildlife Centre.		
5	You are not allowed to swim between the blue flags.		
6	You mustn't take your dog to the beach between May and October.		

Places in your area

2

Are there any places like the ones on the flyers in your area? Talk about them.
Gibt es in eurer Gegend Orte wie die auf den Flyern? Sprecht darüber.

zoo · wildlife park · beach · forest · park · farm · swimming pool · amusement park · ...

swim · have a barbecue · see animals · hire bikes · take your dog · go horse riding · get sandwiches · ...

In my area there is a ...

There you can ...

GRAMMAR HELP

Du hast schon gelernt, dass **Subjekt**, Verb und Objekt in englischen Aussagesätzen immer in einer bestimmten Reihenfolge stehen.

Wie ist es mit **Ortsangaben** *(where)* und mit **Zeitangaben** *(when)*?

Sieh dir die Beispielsätze an. Was fällt dir auf?

You can discover British wildlife **at the British Wildlife Centre** **all year round**.

Visitors mustn't bring dogs **to the beach** **between May and October**.

Parents must watch their children **in the water** **at all times**.

Where and when?

3

Unscramble the sentences and write them down.
Entwirre die Sätze und schreibe sie auf.

1 to the zoo · Let's go · next weekend

Let's go to the zoo next weekend.

2 last Saturday · We · to the British Wildlife Centre · went

3 at the gate · We · are meeting · at 10am · our tour guide

4 before we leave · I · have to buy · online · the tickets

How to say *oo*

5

audio 23

Listen to the words and read along. Then repeat them. What do you notice? Talk about it in German. **Hört euch die Wörter an und lest mit. Wiederholt sie dann. Was fällt euch auf? Sprecht auf Deutsch darüber.**

f**oo**d · g**oo**d · d**oo**r · aftern**oo**n · l**oo**k · c**oo**k · z**oo** · b**oo**k · fl**oo**r

A field trip

6a

Look at the text. What kind of text is it? Tick. ✓
Sieh dir den Text an. Was für eine Art Text ist es? Mache ein Häkchen.

☐ It's a postcard. ☐ It's a text message. ☐ It's a letter.

Holland Park School
Airlie Gardens, Campden Hill Rd
London W8 7AF

To: Year 8 parents

Dear parents,
I'm writing to inform you about our field trip to the British Wildlife Centre on 25th March.
The trip costs £15.00 for each student.
We are leaving by bus from the school's car park at 8am and are coming back at 6pm.
Please make sure that your child is wearing a warm jacket and good shoes for walking.
All students must bring a packed lunch and something to drink.
I am looking forward to an interesting trip!

Yours sincerely,
R. Patel

6b

Find the words and phrases in the text. **Finde die Wörter und Ausdrücke im Text.**

Ausflug	*f* ______	*t* ______	
für jeden Schüler	*f* ______	*e* ______	*s* ______
Schuhe zum Laufen	*s* ______	*f* ______	*w* ______
Lunchpaket	*p* ______	*l* ______	

6c

Read again and match the sentence parts. Write down the sentences.
Lies noch einmal und ordne die Satzteile einander zu. Schreibe dann die Sätze auf.

The year 8 students are	from the school's car park.
They are visiting	going on a field trip.
The bus leaves	the British Wildlife Centre.

At the Wildlife Centre

7a

Look at the pictures. Tick ✓ the two sentences that match the pictures. Sieh dir die Bilder an. Mache ein Häkchen an die zwei Sätze, die zu den Bildern passen.

- ☐ A guide welcomes the students to the Wildlife Centre.
- ☐ A guide welcomes the students in the car park.
- ☐ Mr Patel talks about hedgehogs.
- ☐ A guide talks about hedgehogs.

7b

audio 24

Now listen and read along. Who is Polly? Höre nun zu und lies mit. Wer ist Polly?

Katy: Welcome to the British Wildlife Centre!
I'm Katy, your guide today. My job is to look after the animals here.
I'd like to tell you about animals in Britain and how you can protect them.
Here at the British Wildlife Centre we have over forty different species, for example foxes, squirrels and birds. Today I'm going to show you hedgehogs and bees.
Let's start with the hedgehogs. This way, please.

Katy: This is our hedgehog Polly!
We found her near a busy road and took her to the Wildlife Centre.
Cars are often a problem for hedgehogs. Another problem is that they don't find places where they can live and have enough food. Especially in winter, they need a safe place where they can sleep.
If you have a garden, you can leave areas with long grass and dry leaves for them.
Or you can build a hedgehog house – you only need wood, a hammer and some nails.
Harry: That sounds fun!
Katy: You can also leave food for hedgehogs – cat or dog food is perfect! But you must not give them milk. They only drink water.

7c

Read again. Then match the questions and the answers.

Lies noch einmal. Ordne dann die Fragen und die Antworten einander zu.

1 What is Katy's job?	She shows them the hedgehogs.
2 How many different species are there?	They only drink water.
3 What animals does Katy show the children?	They need a safe place where they can sleep.
4 What do hedgehogs need in winter?	She looks after the animals.
5 Why shouldn't you give hedgehogs milk?	There are over forty species.

7d

Answer the questions. You can find help in the box.

Beantworte die Fragen. Du kannst im Kasten Hilfe finden.

Why do hedgehogs need help? ______________________________

____

What do they eat and drink? ______________________________

____

How can you help them? ______________________________

____

They like areas with long grass. · Cars are a problem for hedgehogs. · Hedgehogs are brown. · They like cat and dog food. · I can build a hedgehog house. · I can leave food for them. · Hedgehogs only drink water. · It's a problem for hedgehogs to find a place to stay in winter.

LAND & LEUTE 5 video 8

Tiere an der britischen Küste

Im Vereinigten Königreich kann man vor allem an der Küste viele Tiere sehen, die man dort nicht erwartet.

Tümmler werden regelmäßig gesichtet. Sie leben in kleinen Gruppen von bis zu 15 Tieren. Auch gewöhnliche Schweinswale tauchen häufig an der Küste auf. Selbst Lederschildkröten kann man zwischen Mai und September manchmal entdecken.

In den Gewässern des Vereinigten Königreichs gibt es sogar über 40 verschiedene Arten von Haien, unter anderem den Riesenhai, den zweitgrößten Fisch der Welt.

Sieh dir den Videoclip an.
Was findest du überraschend?

Wildlife

8a

Read the text. Underline what you think is interesting. Lies den Text. Unterstreiche, was du interessant findest.

Did you know that the largest fish in British waters are basking sharks? They can be up to 11m long and weigh up to 7 tonnes. That is nearly the same weight as a London double-decker bus!
Basking sharks are the second largest fish in the world! You can see them between May and August near the coast of Cornwall. They swim slowly near the surface with their mouths wide open, filtering plankton from the water to eat.

basking shark = Riesenhai

8b

Complete the sentences. Present the basking shark to the class.
Vervollständige die Sätze. Stelle der Klasse den Riesenhai vor.

The largest *fish in British waters are basking sharks.*

They can be up to ______________ and they can weigh ______________

Basking sharks are the ______________

You can see them between ______________

They swim with their mouths ______________

A mini project

10a

Look at the pictures. What are the instructions for?
Sieh dir die Bilder an. Für was sind die Anleitungen?

- ☐ a hedgehog house
- ☐ a bird feeder
- ☐ an insect hotel

MAKE YOUR OWN BIRD FEEDER

You need:
fat, nuts, a yoghurt pot, string

1. Mix the fat and the nuts.
2. Put them inside the yoghurt pot.
3. Put the string around the yoghurt pot.
4. Hang it in a tree where you can watch the birds.

10b

Your little sister wants to make a bird feeder. Tell her in German what to do.
Deine kleine Schwester möchte eine Vogelfutterstation machen. Sage ihr auf Deutsch, was sie machen muss.

Zuerst mischst du die Nüsse und …

A Notting Hill environment project

11a audio 25

Listen to the interview and read along. **Höre dir das Interview an und lies mit.**

Reporter: Hello and welcome to today's radio show "London Neighbourhoods". I am Trevor and with me are Tarek and Lily from Notting Hill. Tarek, what are you doing here?
Tarek: Hi. Well, we're planting flowers here. We were at the British Wildlife Centre for our school trip last week and we got some ideas for mini projects. Right now our friends Ava and Harry are putting seeds in the ground.
Reporter: It looks quite interesting. Lily, why are you planting those flowers here?
Lily: We're trying to help bees and butterflies. They don't find enough to eat in the city.

11b

Can you answer these questions? Underline the answers in the text in the colour of the questions. **Kannst du diese Fragen beantworten? Unterstreiche die Antworten im Text in der Farbe der Fragen.**
Who is Trevor? What are the flowers for? What are the children doing? Who is there?

Garden arts and crafts

12a

What do you need to build a hedgehog house? Number the words.
Was brauchst du, um ein Igelhaus zu bauen? Nummeriere die Wörter.

1

2

3

4

6

5

nails ☐	dry grass ☐	wood 1	earth ☐	hammer ☐	leaves ☐

12b

Read the sentences. Number them in the right order and copy them.
Lies die Sätze. Nummeriere sie in der richtigen Reihenfolge und schreibe sie ab.

☐ Then put the house in a quiet place in your garden.

1 To make a hedgehog house you need: wood, hammer, nails.

☐ To finish your hedgehog house, put some dry grass and leaves inside and cover it with earth.

☐ First, build a small house out of the wood.

A spelling exercise

13 audio 26

Listen to the words and repeat them. Complete the table.
Höre dir die Wörter an und wiederhole sie. Vervollständige die Tabelle.

knife	leaf	shelf	wife	half
knives		shelves		

What do you notice? Talk about it. **Was fällt euch auf? Sprecht darüber.**

Our environment brochure TARGET TASK

14

Create a page for an environment brochure.
Entwirf eine Seite für eine Umweltbroschüre.

Step 1

The idea is to make an insect hotel to help the environment.
An insect hotel can help because many insects ...

- don't have a place to stay
- need a dry place to build a nest
- ...

Step 2

What do we need? Read and match. Was brauchen wir? Lies und ordne zu.

string

bark

pine cones

stones

moss

toilet paper rolls

plastic bottle

sticks

Step 3

How do we make it? Find the right order. Copy the text and design your page.
Wie machen wir es? Finde die richtige Reihenfolge. Schreibe den Text ab und entwirf deine Seite.

____ Then add pieces of toilet paper roll, some sticks and some pine cones.

____ Put the string around the bottle.

__1__ Cut the bottle into two parts so that you can make two hotels.

____ Hang it up in a safe place.

____ First fill it with some moss, stones and bark.

Rules at school

Read the sentences and fill in *must* or *mustn't*.
Lies die Sätze und trage *must* oder *mustn't* ein.

1 All students ______________ wear the correct school uniform.

2 They ______________ only eat in the cafeteria.

3 The students ______________ use their mobile phones in class.

4 They ______________ talk during tests.

5 They ______________ always do their homework.

6 The students ______________ run in the school building.

7 They ______________ play ball games in the classroom.

8 The teachers ______________ arrive late for their lessons.

Mum, can I …?

Read the sentences and answer them for yourself.
Lies die Sätze und beantworte sie für dich.

Yes, you can. · No, you can't.

1 Mum, can I watch a horror film tonight? *No, you can't.*

2 Can I visit my friends on Saturday? ______________

3 Can I wear make-up at school? ______________

4 Mum, can I come home after 10 o'clock? ______________

5 Can I play football before I do my homework? ______________

6 Can I wear my old jeans to Grandma's birthday party? ______________

Jobs at home

What must the people do before they can do something else? Write sentences.
Was müssen die Leute tun, bevor sie etwas anderes tun können? Schreibe Sätze.

1

2

3

4

5

6

1 clean the cage / watch TV *The girl must clean the cage.*
Then she can watch TV.

2 empty the dishwasher / read a book

3 take out the rubbish / watch a film

4 clean the bathroom / play with his children

5 go shopping / go swimming

6 set the table / play computer games after dinner

Important words

So sagst du, was jemand tun oder nicht tun darf:

So kannst du Insekten und Igeln helfen:

I can build ...

Diese Wörter aus diesem Kapitel fand ich interessant:

4

The future

1 What can you see in the picture? Collect words.
2 What do you think: what are the children's ideas about their future?

Part A My dreams

- Du lernst, über Zukunftsträume zu sprechen.
- Du sprichst über Berufswünsche.
- Du präsentierst deine Ideen über die Zukunft.

Part B Stories

- Du liest die Geschichte *Kate and Jonathan's adventure*.
- Du lernst, was Texte lebendiger und interessanter machen kann.
- Du schreibst eine eigene kurze Geschichte.

A time capsule project

1a

Read the flyer. What is the project about?
Lies das Flugblatt. Worum geht es in dem Projekt?

What will the future bring?
What are your dreams?

TAKE PART IN OUR SCIENCE MUSEUM TIME CAPSULE PROJECT!

????

What do you think: what will life be like in 20 years' time?
What will the world look like?
What are your dreams for the future?

Write about your ideas about the future, draw your ideas, paint them or film them.

How will we live, work, eat, learn, travel, ...?

We will put your works in a time capsule. There will be a public opening of the capsule in 20 years.

Please hand in your work by 26 May online or at the museum!

1b

What is a time capsule? Tick. ✓ Was ist eine Zeitkapsel? Mache ein Häkchen.

☐ In einer Zeitkapsel sind Gegenstände oder Kunstwerke aus der Gegenwart. Sie soll in der Zukunft geöffnet werden.

☐ In einer Zeitkapsel ist eine schöne Uhr, die immer die richtige Zeit anzeigt, auch in der Zukunft.

Ideas about the future

2a

Look at the picture. What is Lily doing? Schau dir das Bild an. Was tut Lily gerade?

☐ Lily is reading. ☐ Lily is working on a collage. ☐ Lily is cleaning her room.

2b audio 27

Listen and read along. What jobs do the children talk about?
Höre dir den Text an und lies mit. Über welche Berufe sprechen die Kinder?

d ____________ e ____________ s ____________ c ____________

Ava: Hi Lily, what are you doing?
Lily: Hi guys. I am working on a collage for this project at the Science Museum about the future. You can make a drawing, a film, a poem or a story. There'll be an exhibition and they'll keep 15 works in a time capsule. In 20 years, there will be a public opening.
Ava: Cool!
Harry: OK Lily, so where will you be in 20 years? Still in this room? Haha ...
Lily: Very funny, Harry. No, I won't. I'll live in New York, and I'll be a famous fashion designer. What about your plans, guys?
Ava: I want to be an engineer when I grow up. I'll invent lots of useful things to help people.
Harry: I won't have a regular job. I'll be a really famous singer.
Lily: Phew! You can sing, Harry – but it's loud and not good. Tarek, where will you be in 20 years?
Tarek: I'll be the best chef in London and have my own restaurant!
Ava: Great – and we'll be your best customers!
Lily: Guys, I have a great idea: why don't you all take part in the project, too?
Ava: That's a cool idea, Lily! But I think we should write about technology and food and houses, not just our jobs.
Tarek: I'll draw some food from the future!
Harry: I'll record a song. Then I can include my guitar playing!
Ava: And I'll do something about technology in the future. Brilliant!

2c

Match the sentence parts. Verbinde die Satzteile.

1 There is a project	a collage for the project.
2 Lily is making	at the Science Museum.
3 The museum will put some works	is to be a fashion designer.
4 Lily's dream for the future	in a time capsule.
5 Harry wants to	be a chef.
6 Ava wants to	be a singer.
7 Tarek wants to	be an engineer.

2d

What would you put in a time capsule? You can draw or write something.
Was würdest du in eine Zeitkapsel tun? Du kannst etwas zeichnen oder schreiben.

GRAMMAR HELP

Wenn du über die Zukunft sprechen möchtest, kannst du das *will-future* verwenden.
Sieh dir die Beispielsätze an.

There **will be** an exhibition. → Es **wird** eine Ausstellung **geben**.
We'**ll be** your best customers. → Wir **werden** deine besten Kunden **sein**.
I **will not be** in this room in 20 years. → Ich **werde** in 20 Jahren **nicht** in diesem Raum **sein**.
I **won't have** a regular job. → Ich **werde keinen** normalen Beruf **haben**.

Future jobs

3

Match the sentences from the box to the statements and write them down.
Ordne die Sätze aus dem Kasten den Aussagen zu und schreibe sie auf.

~~You'll be a chef.~~ · You'll be a fashion designer. · You'll be an engineer. · You'll be a famous singer.

1 I enjoy cooking. *You'll be a chef.*
2 I love music. ______
3 I like fancy clothes. ______
4 I want to invent useful things. ______

When I grow up

4

Look at the pictures and write about the children's ideas for the future.
Sieh dir die Bilder an und schreibe, welche Ideen die Kinder für die Zukunft haben.

George *will be married* and he will ______.
Ahmed will ______.

He will ______.
He won't ______.

Anna ______.
She ______.
She ______.

~~be married~~ · have many children · be a teacher · ride a bike · drive a car · be a singer · work in an office · have a family

People at work

6a

What jobs do you know? Circle the words.
Welche Berufe kennst du? Kreise die Wörter ein.

pilot · baker · nurse · police officer · mechanic · teacher · doctor · gardener · firefighter · shop assistant · ...

6b

Look at the photos. What do these people do in their jobs?
Schau dir die Fotos an. Was machen diese Leute in ihren Berufen?

firefighter

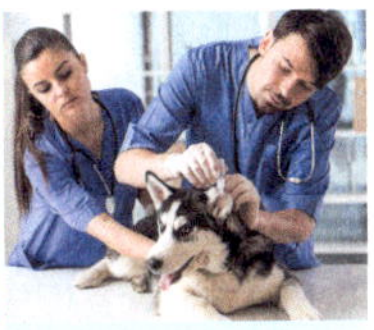
vet

police officer

nurse

computer game designer

hairdresser

A firefighter *fights fires and helps people and animals.*

A police officer ______

cuts and colours people's hair · takes care of ill people · helps people in trouble and arrests criminals · ~~fights fires and helps people and animals~~ · designs computer games · takes care of ill animals

6c

Which words match the two jobs? Write them down. Add more.
Welche Wörter passen zu den zwei Berufen? Schreibe sie auf. Füge weitere hinzu.

hospital · ~~fashion~~ · ill people · colour · doctor · customers · patients · stand a lot · walk a lot · broken leg · fever · ...

hairdresser: fashion,

nurse:

An interview

7a

Look at the picture of Mehti. He is working. What do you think his job is? Tick ✓. Sieh dir das Bild von Mehti an. Er arbeitet. Was ist wohl sein Beruf? Mache ein Häkchen.

I think Mehti is working as ☐ a nurse. ☐ an influencer. ☐ a police officer.

7b audio 28

Listen to the podcast. How does Mehti earn his money? Höre dir den Podcast an. Wie verdient Mehti sein Geld?

7c

Look at the statements about Mehti's job. Circle the right words. Sieh dir die Aussagen über Mehtis Job an. Kreise die richtigen Wörter ein.

1 Mehti packt die Sachen vor der Kamera **aus / ein** und **verändert / beschreibt** sie.

2 Viele Leute **bedanken / beschweren** sich bei Mehti für seine Arbeit.

3 Oft haben Leute einfach keine **Lust / Zeit**, in einen Laden zu gehen.

4 Die **Firmen / Kunden** schicken Mehti oft Dinge zum **Einpacken / Auspacken**.

5 Mehti verdient sein Geld mit **Werbung / Spenden**.

A job quiz

8a

Who does what? Answer the questions. Wer macht was? Beantworte die Fragen.

That's a nurse. · That's a hairdresser. · That's a shop assistant. · That's a vet.

1 Who helps you when you want to buy something in a shop?

____

2 Who washes and cuts your hair? _______________

3 Who looks after you when you are in a hospital? _______________

4 Who looks after your pet when it is ill? _______________

8b

Find the matching questions to the answers and copy them.
Finde die passenden Fragen zu den Antworten und schreibe sie ab.

Who bakes bread? · Who arrests criminals? · Who fights fires?

______________________________ 1 That's a police officer.

______________________________ 2 That's a firefighter.

______________________________ 3 That's a baker.

Our dream jobs

9a

Match the German and the English words.
Verbinde die deutschen und die englischen Wörter.

photographer	chef	baker	zoologist	vet	pilot
Koch / Köchin	Fotograf / Fotografin	Zoologe / Zoologin	Pilot / Pilotin	Bäcker / Bäckerin	Tierarzt / Tierärztin

9b

video 10, media worksheet A

Watch the video clip. Who wants to have which job? Make sentences and write them down. Sieh dir das Video an. Wer möchte welchen Beruf haben? Bilde Sätze und schreibe sie auf.

Lewis Rosa Eran George	wants to be	a vet or a zoologist. a chef. a pilot. a photographer or a baker.

____

____

____

____

Joshua's questions

11a audio 29

Listen to Joshua and Ava. What are they talking about? Tick ✓.
Höre Joshua und Ava zu. Worüber reden sie? Mache ein Häkchen.

They are talking about ☐ their favourite food. ☐ music. ☐ their future.

11b audio 29

Listen again. Write down Ava's answers to Joshua's questions.
Höre noch einmal zu. Schreibe Avas Antworten auf Joshuas Fragen auf.

Of course! · Yes, I will. I'll invent a lot of useful things. · I'll be an engineer.

1 What will you be when you grow up? ______

2 Will you invent really cool things? ______

3 Will you still need your skateboard? ______

Tell me about your future

12a

Read the three questions and match them with the German questions.
Lies die drei Fragen und verbinde sie mit den deutschen Fragen.

1 What will be your job?	Wie viele Kinder wirst du haben?
2 Where will you live?	Wo wirst du wohnen?
3 How many children will you have?	Welchen Beruf wirst du haben?

12b

Answer the questions for yourself. **Beantworte die Fragen für dich.**

1 I will be ______
a baker/an actress / a police officer/...

2 I will live ______
on Mars / at home / in New York / in a villa / ...

3 I will have ______
one child / no children / two children / ... children.

Lily's predictions

13a

Read Lily's predictions. Underline what she says about school in the future.
Lies Lilys Vorhersagen. Unterstreiche, was sie über Schule in der Zukunft sagt.

In 20 years there won't be any more cars. People will ride their bikes or fly solar-powered helicopters.

At school the students won't have exercise books or pens and pencils anymore. They can read and write on their tablets and learn with VR glasses.

TVs will be even bigger than today. Or maybe there won't be any TVs and people will watch holograms in their living rooms.

13b

Sort the words from the box into the table.
Ordne die Wörter aus dem Kasten in die Tabelle ein.

no cars · no exercise books · solar-powered helicopters · tablets · VR glasses · bikes · no pens · watch holograms

travel	at school	at home

In the future, there will be ...

14 audio 30

Listen to the song and sing along.
Höre dir das Lied an und singe mit.

In the future, there will be a lot of robots,
lot of robots, lot of robots,
in the future, there will be a lot of robots.
Oh, the future will be really wonderful!

The future

15

What do you think about the future? Write down questions and then add the answers. Was denkst du über die Zukunft? Schreibe Fragen auf und füge dann die Antworten hinzu.

Will robots do	vegetarians?	Yes, they will.
Will we still	all our chores?	No, they won't.
Will people live	have cars?	Yes, we will.
Will we all be	on the moon?	No, we won't.

1.
2.
3.
4.

Odd one out

16a

Find the odd one out and underline it.
Finde das Wort, das nicht zu den anderen passt, und unterstreiche es.

1 car, bus, plane, bike
2 hairdresser, daughter, baker, photographer
3 computer, book, tablet, mobile phone
4 living room, library, science lab, cafeteria

16b

Can you say why it is the odd one out? Write the matching number from 16a next to the sentence. Kannst du sagen, warum das Wort nicht passt? Schreibe die passende Zahl aus 16a neben den Satz.

☐ *It is paper.*

☐ *It is not a job.*

☐ *It is not at school.*

☐ *It can fly.*

My ideas about the future TARGET TASK

18 media worksheet C

Your task is to present your ideas about the future. You can draw and write.

Deine Aufgabe ist, deine Vorstellungen von der Zukunft zu präsentieren. Du kannst zeichnen und schreiben.

JOBS
(Hier kannst du schreiben oder zeichnen, was man in der Zukunft arbeitet.)

FOOD
(Hier kannst du schreiben oder zeichnen, was man in der Zukunft isst.)

THE FUTURE

SCHOOL
(Hier kannst du schreiben oder zeichnen, was man in der Zukunft in der Schule macht.)

HOUSES
(Hier kannst du schreiben oder zeichnen, wie man in der Zukunft wohnt.)

Kate and Jonathan's adventure – part one

1a

Look at the pictures. What sentence goes with the story?

Schau dir die Bilder an. Welcher Satz passt zu der Geschichte?

☐ Kate and Jonathan are planning a party.

☐ Kate and Jonathan discover a tunnel in the cellar.

☐ Kate and Jonathan are cleaning the house at night.

1b

Read the story. Where are Kate and Jonathan? What do they discover?

Lies den ersten Teil der Geschichte.

Wo sind Kate und Jonathan? Was entdecken sie?

1c

Complete the sentences. **Ergänze die Sätze.**

1 Jonathan showed his new watch to his best ______________ Kate.
2 Kate was not ______________ interested.
3 Kate had an ______________.
4 She wanted to go to the old ______________.
5 They walked down the stairs and found a ______________.

very · friend · cellar · tunnel · idea

1d

What do you think: what will happen next? Write down your ideas.
Was denkst du: Was wird als nächstes passieren? Schreibe deine Ideen auf.

Next, Jonathan will ______________________________.

They will find ______________________________.

GRAMMAR HELP

Du kennst bereits Adjektive zum Beschreiben von Personen, Tieren oder Sachen. Wenn du beschreiben willst, **wie jemand etwas tut** oder **wie etwas geschieht**, benutzt du ein Adverb der Art und Weise *(adverb of manner)*. Vergleiche die Sätze und Wörter. Was fällt dir auf?

Kate was **polite**.	She looked at the watch **politely**.	**polite** + **ly** = **politely**
The children were **careful**.	They walked **carefully** down the stairs.	**careful** + **ly** = **carefully**

Einige wenige *adverbs of manner* haben unregelmäßige Formen, z. B. **good** → **well** und **fast** → **fast**.

What is it like?

2a

Match the adjectives with the adverbs. Then write down the pairs.

Ordne die Adjektive den Adverbien zu. Schreibe dann die Paare auf.

adjectives	adverbs
careful	happily
fast	slowly
good	loudly
happy	fast
slow	carefully
sad	beautifully
beautiful	sadly
loud	well

careful – carefully

______

______

______

______

______

______

______

2b

Read the sentences and add an adverb from 2a.

Lies die Sätze und füge ein Adverb aus 2a hinzu.

1 The man is driving *carefully*.

2 The dog is running ______.

3 The girl is singing ______.

4 The boys are playing ______.

5 The woman is working ______.

Kate and Jonathan's adventure – part two

4a

audio 31

Listen to the next part of the story. What is happening? Tick ✓.
Höre dir den nächsten Teil der Geschichte an. Was passiert? Mache ein Häkchen.

- [ ] Kate und Jonathan räumen den Keller auf.
- [ ] Kate und Jonathan rutschen in die Zukunft.
- [ ] Kate und Jonathan machen das Licht an.

4b

audio 31

Listen again. Find the right sentence endings and circle them. Write down the sentences. **Höre noch einmal zu. Finde die richtigen Satzenden und kreise sie ein. Schreibe die Sätze auf.**

1 Jonathan goes **down a tunnel** / **down the river on a boat**.
2 When Jonathan comes out of the tunnel he sees **Kate** / **a tiger**.
3 Kate finds it all **really scary** / **really exciting**.
4 In the end, the children find out that they are **in the future** / **in another town**.

____

____

____

____

4c

What do you think: how do Kate and Jonathan feel? Match the English and the German words. **Was denkst du: Wie fühlen sich Kate und Jonathan? Ordne die englischen und die deutschen Wörter einander zu.**

excited · scared · happy · bored · terrible · sick · surprised · worried · good · bad

schlecht · gut · besorgt · überrascht · übel · schrecklich · gelangweilt · fröhlich · ängstlich · aufgeregt

I think Jonathan feels ______________________________.

I think Kate feels ______________________________.

Kate and Jonathan's adventure – part three

5a

Look at the pictures. What do you think: how will the story end?
Schau dir die Bilder an. Was glaubst du: Wie wird die Geschichte enden?

☐ They find a friend and can go home. ☐ They find a friend and stay in the future.

5b

Read part three of the story. What happens to Kate and Jonathan?
Lies Teil drei der Geschichte. Was passiert Kate und Jonathan?

What now?

1 The children were quiet for a moment. Their first idea was to walk back into the tunnel and go back. That did not work. Then they walked towards Kate's house – but there was a different house. "Oh dear. We really ARE in the future." Jonathan said.

____

2 A girl came out. "Hi," Kate said. "I'm Kate. And over there is Jonathan. We're from the past." The girl smiled. "Kate! I'm Georgia. I got a letter from you. I found it and this strange thing in a corner at the back of the old cellar. Wait, let me get it." She ran to the house.

____

3 A few minutes later, Georgia was back. She showed them a small thing. "That's my grandfather's old compass," Kate said. "Look," Georgia said. There was a letter inside the compass. "Here's your letter. It says that you can only travel here if you are the owner of the compass. The compass will also get you back to your time." "Oh, thank God! We can go back home," Jonathan said.

____

4 "Can you tell us all about the future first, Georgia?" "Sure," Georgia said. Georgia told Kate and Jonathan about solar-powered transport, smart homes and virtual

teachers. The future sounded like a good place, Kate and Jonathan thought. They told Georgia about their school and how they travelled there by bus every morning.

____

5 Later they went back through the tunnel with the compass. A few seconds later they were back in Kate's old cellar. "OK," Jonathan said. "Now we have to write that letter to Georgia and hide it together with the compass in the cellar, so that Georgia can find it in the future?" "Yes," Kate said. "And one day we should visit Georgia again. Maybe she wants to come back with us for a visit."

5c

Find the matching headings to the paragraphs in 5b. Write them down.
Finde die passenden Überschriften zu den Absätzen in 5b. Schreibe sie auf.

Going home · A letter from the past ·
Meeting Georgia · Life in the future · ~~What now?~~

5d

What happens in this part of the story? Match the sentence parts.
Was passiert in diesem Teil der Geschichte? Verbinde die Satzteile.

1 Kate and Jonathan try to go back, but they	future.
2 They meet Georgia, a friendly girl from the	letter.
3 Georgia gives them a compass that helps them to go	can't.
4 Kate and Jonathan go home and write the	home.

Your opinion

6

What do you like about the story? **Was magst du an der Geschichte?**

I like

Kate ☆☆☆☆☆
Jonathan ☆☆☆☆☆

I like ______________ because ______________.

Georgia ☆☆☆☆☆
the future ☆☆☆☆☆

I like ______________ because ______________.

the compass ☆☆☆☆☆
the letter ☆☆☆☆☆

I like ______________ because ______________.

The story

7

Think about the story again. Write one or two sentences about the three parts in German. You can use the prompts from the boxes.
Denke noch einmal über die Geschichte nach. Schreibe auf Deutsch ein oder zwei Sätze über die drei Teile. Du kannst die Stichworte aus den Kästen benutzen.

Teil 1: Armbanduhr · Lampe · Keller · Tunnel · Freunde · verschwunden

Teil 2: Tunnel · Rutsche · Kate · aufregend · Zukunft · ...

Teil 3: Haus · Georgia · Brief · Kompass · Gespräch · zurück nach Hause

Good style

8a

Look at the words. Match them to their German meaning.
Sieh dir die Wörter an. Ordne sie ihrer deutschen Bedeutung zu.

friendly · angry · sunny · cold · old · red · tall · new · dangerous · exciting

alt · gefährlich · kalt · wütend · freundlich · rot · groß · aufregend · sonnig · neu

8b

Write down the adjectives that go with the nouns. There can be more than one possibility. **Schreibe die Adjektive auf, die zu den Hauptwörtern passen. Es kann mehr als eine Möglichkeit geben.**

people: ____________________

weather: ____________________

buildings: ____________________

situations: ____________________

Past, present or future?

10a

video 11, media worksheet A

Watch the video clip. Which child wants to travel into the future?

Sieh dir den Videoclip an. Welches Kind möchte in die Zukunft reisen?

10b

Work in a small group. Interview each other.

Arbeitet in einer Kleingruppe. Befragt euch gegenseitig.

	name:	name:	name:
1 What time would you like to travel to?			
2 Who would you like to meet?			
3 What would you take with you?			
4 What would you do there?			

1 *I would like to travel to the future / the past / the year ...*

2 *I would like to meet ...*

3 *I would like to take my ... with me.*

4 *I would ... there.*

LAND & LEUTE 6 video 12

Science-Fiction

Bücher und Filme, die Maschinen mit hoher künstlicher Intelligenz, Raumfahrt, Roboter oder Begegnungen mit Außerirdischen zum Thema haben, nennt man Science-Fiction. Die ältesten dieser Bücher sind über 200 Jahre alt. Berühmte Autoren sind Jules Verne und H. G. Wells. H. G. Wells beschrieb schon 1895 in seinem Roman *The time machine* eine Reise in die Zukunft mithilfe einer Zeitmaschine.

Vor allem seit den 1960er Jahren sind auch Filme zu dem Thema sehr beliebt. Besonders bekannt sind die Filme *Back to the future 1*, *2* und *3* des Regisseurs Steven Spielberg. In den Filmen reist ein Jugendlicher mit einem zur Zeitmaschine umgebauten Auto durch die Zeit.

Welche Science-Fiction-Filme, -Comics oder -Bücher kennst du?

Linking words

12a

Look at the words. Match them with the German words.
Schau dir die Wörter an. Verbinde sie mit den deutschen Wörtern.

so that · because · but · and · before · when

weil · damit · aber · bevor · als · und

12b

Make one sentence out of two. Use words from 12a. Write down the sentences.
Mache aus zwei Sätzen einen. Verwende Wörter aus 12a. Schreibe die Sätze auf.

1 Olivia tried to take a picture of the dinosaur. Her camera did not work.

____

2 In the year 2070 people won't travel by car. They won't travel by bus.

____

3 Mia was surprised. She found out that she was in the year 2812.

____

Improve your text

13

Complete the beginning of this story with a word from the brackets.
Vervollständige den Anfang dieser Geschichte mit einem Wort aus den Klammern.

It was a ______________ (sunny / rainy) Monday morning. Buzz woke up ______________ (really / very) early. He was ______________ (very / terribly) excited. Today was his ______________ (big / special) day ______________ (and / so) he couldn't wait to get up.

My story TARGET TASK

14 media worksheet C

Your task is to write a short story about a time travelling adventure. You can use the table to help you. Deine Aufgabe ist, eine kurze Geschichte über ein Zeitreise-Abenteuer zu schreiben. Du kannst die Tabelle als Hilfe benutzen.

Part	My text:	Was du schreiben kannst:
The beginning		Schreibe hier auf, wo deine Geschichte spielt und wer dabei ist. – It all started in a **big city** / **at home** / **...** – **Nicole** / **Tim** / **...** woke up and ...
The time travel		Schreibe hier auf, wie deine Hauptfigur in die Zukunft reist. – Suddenly there was **a loud noise** / **a bright light** / **a tunnel in the wall** / **...**
The future		Schreibe hier auf, wie es in der Zukunft aussieht und wer dort ist. – **The houses were** / **...** – It was **dangerous** / **nice** / **terrible** / **...** because there were ...
The way home		Schreibe hier, wie deine Hauptfigur den Weg zurück findet. – **A girl** / **...** told **her** / **him** to **go to the mountain** / **sing a song** / **say a magic word ...**
Home again		Schreibe hier, wie deine Hauptfigur von der Reise erzählt und wie sie sich fühlt. – At home, **she** / **he** told **her** / **his mum** / **dad** / **brother** / **...** about ...

What will they have?

1

Look at the table and write about Sara and Brad.

Sieh dir die Tabelle an und schreibe über Sara und Brad.

	Leon	Sara	Brad
have a family	(+)	(-)	(+)
live in a big city	(+)	(+)	(-)
have a regular job	(-)	(-)	(+)
live alone	(-)	(+)	(-)

Leon will have a family and he will live in a big city.
Leon won't have a regular job and he won't live alone.

Sara won't have ______________________________

She will live ______________________________

Brad ______________________________

He ______________________________

What job is this?

2

Match the sentences to the jobs. There can be more than one possibility.

Ordne die Sätze den Berufen zu. Es kann mehr als eine Möglichkeit geben.

Your work can be dangerous.	firefighter	You work with animals.
You work in a team.	police officer	You help pets.
You help people in trouble.	computer game designer	You work outside.
You wear a uniform.		You work alone.
You work a lot with computers.	nurse	You know a lot about fashion.
You work in a hospital.	hairdresser	You work inside.
You help ill people.	vet	You cut people's hair.

Adverbs

3a

Find the 12 adverbs → ↓ and write them into the list. Add the adjectives that go with them. Look at page 92 for help.

Finde die 12 Adverbien → ↓ und schreibe sie in die Liste. Füge die Adjektive hinzu, die dazu passen. Sieh dir Seite 92 an, wenn du Hilfe brauchst.

A	B	E	A	U	T	I	F	U	L	L	Y	S	T
B	N	S	L	P	S	A	E	R	U	T	S	S	E
P	E	R	Q	U	I	C	K	L	Y	R	E	A	R
R	D	H	F	G	U	O	S	P	A	U	I	D	R
O	C	A	R	E	F	U	L	L	Y	P	D	L	I
U	H	P	U	Z	A	N	O	D	S	I	L	Y	B
D	F	P	O	H	S	E	W	F	I	S	O	A	L
L	U	I	T	C	T	L	L	O	U	D	L	Y	Y
Y	S	L	Q	I	G	B	Y	Z	N	S	K	O	U
F	C	Y	U	K	D	S	H	T	W	E	L	L	N
D	A	N	G	E	R	O	U	S	L	Y	N	I	A
K	I	H	E	N	C	O	F	T	K	P	U	O	T

beautifully	*beautiful*		

3b

Complete the sentences with a matching adverb.

Vervollständige die Sätze mit einem passenden Adverb.

My mum bakes a cake ______________________.

My sister plays the guitar ______________________.

We work ______________________.

I do my homework ______________________.

My uncle drives his car ______________________.

A singer sings ______________________.

Important words

Sätze, um über die Zukunft zu sprechen:

I will be …

I won't be …

I will have …

Jobs:

firefighter,

Adjektive und Adverbien, die ich mir merken will:

5

Out and about

1 Look at the picture. What can you see?
2 Where are the people?

Part A A trip to the museum

- Du beschäftigst dich mit interessanten Museen in London.
- Du übst, Dinge zu beschreiben.
- Du beschreibst Dinge für eine Ausstellung.

Part B A play

- Du unterhältst dich über Ferien.
- Du lernst die Geschichte *The Canterville Ghost* kennen.
- Du spielst mit einer Gruppe eine kurze Szene aus einem Theaterstück vor.

A place to visit

1

Look at the list of places to go. Circle what is interesting to you. Talk to a partner. **Sieh dir die Liste der Orte an, zu denen man gehen kann. Kreise ein, was für dich interessant ist. Sprecht zu zweit.**

a science museum · a train museum · an old castle · a shopping centre · a zoo · a halfpipe · a stadium

I'd like to visit a train museum.
You can see … there.

I want to see …
You can learn about …

Museums in London

2a

Read the flyer. What museums is it about?
Lies die Broschüre. Von welchen Museen handelt sie?

DISCOVER LONDON'S MUSEUMS

THE BRITISH MUSEUM
At the British Museum you can learn how to write your name in hieroglyphs. Or have a look at the mummy of a cat that is more than 4,000 years old.

THE VICTORIA AND ALBERT MUSEUM
From 3,000-year-old Egyptian shoes to modern trainers – they have collected more than 2,000 pairs of shoes.

THE SHERLOCK HOLMES MUSEUM
Do you like detective stories? At the Sherlock Holmes Museum you can step right into the house of the most famous detective of them all: Sherlock Holmes.

2b

Which of the three museums would you like to visit? Say why.
Welche der drei Museen würdest du gern besuchen? Sage, warum.

... it is interesting. · ... I like detective stories. · ... I'd like to see the old shoes. · ... I have never seen a mummy. · ...

I'd like to visit the …
because …

Let's do something different!

3a audio 32

Listen and read along. **Höre zu und lies mit.**

The children are at Harry and Lily's place.

Harry: I've just looked at my weather app – rain for the rest of the day. Any ideas what we could do?
Lily: Look at this flyer for museums in London. They have put together lots of interesting information on museums.
Ava: Museums? That's boring.
Lily: No, no, no, wait. Look. There's a collection of shoes at the V&A! Have you ever seen a shoe that's 3,000 years old?
Ava: No, I haven't. It's probably really smelly.
Lily: Well, we can always stay at home but why not try something different?
Harry: Wow, the British Museum looks really good.
Lily: There are real mummies! Have you ever seen a mummy?
Tarek: Yes, I have.
Ava: Here's something else – the Sherlock Holmes Museum at Baker Street.
Harry: Oh! We've read a story about him at school. He was a clever detective. Let's go there. I want to see what the real home of Sherlock Holmes looks like.
Lily: Harry, you know he's just a character from a book, don't you? He didn't really live in that house.
Harry: Erm ... of course I do.

3b

Read the dialogue again. Complete the sentences.
Lies den Dialog noch einmal. Vervollständige die Sätze.

museums are boring · clever detective · flyer · the British Museum · is probably smelly

1 Lily shows her friends a ______________________.
2 At first Ava says that ______________________.
3 A 3,000-year-old shoe ______________________.
4 Harry has never been to ______________________.
5 Sherlock Holmes was a ______________________.

GRAMMAR HELP

Wenn du über etwas sprechen möchtest, das irgendwann in der Vergangenheit angefangen oder stattgefunden hat und immer noch Einfluss auf die Gegenwart hat, verwendest du das *present perfect*. Schau dir die Beispiele an.

I **have** just **looked** at my weather app.	Ich **habe** gerade auf meine Wetter-App **geschaut**.
We **have**n't **watched** the film yet.	Wir **haben** den Film noch nicht **gesehen**.
Lily **has found** a flyer.	Lily **hat** einen Flyer **gefunden**.
Lily **has**n't **seen** a real mummy yet.	Lily **hat** bisher noch keine echte Mumie **gesehen**.

Ist dir aufgefallen, dass die Verbformen sehr unterschiedlich gebildet werden? Merke dir: **Regelmäßige Verben** wie look, visit, watch, ... erhalten zusätzlich zu **have/has** die Endung **-ed**. Bei **unregelmäßigen Verben** wie be, do, see, ... musst du zusätzlich zu **have/has** die unregelmäßige 3. Form zufügen. Du kannst sie auch in der Liste auf den Seiten 146 und 147 nachschlagen.

What have they done?

4

Fill in the gaps with the correct verb forms from the box.
Fülle die Lücken mit den richtigen Verbformen aus dem Kasten aus.

seen · been · read · watched · found

1 Ava has ______________ (**be**) to a lot of museums.

2 Lily has ______________ (**find**) a flyer about museums in London.

3 Tarek has already ______________ (**see**) a real mummy.

4 Harry has ______________ (**read**) detective stories at school.

5 Noah has ______________ (**watch**) a lot of Sherlock Holmes films.

Been there, done that

5

Paul is on holiday in London. What has he already done? What hasn't he done yet? Write about it. **Paul ist in London in Urlaub. Was hat er schon gemacht? Was hat er noch nicht gemacht? Schreibe darüber.**

Paul **hasn't** *visited* the Science Museum yet.	☐ visit the Science Museum
He **has** *watched* a musical.	☑ watch a musical
He **hasn't** ______________	☐ find a souvenir for Grandma
He **has** ______________	☑ call Mum

At the Sherlock Holmes Museum

6a

audio 33

Listen and read along. Höre zu und lies mit.

Lily: OK, here are your tickets. Let's start.
Harry: Great, thanks Lily.
Tarek: This really looks like someone's home.
Ava: Yes, it does. Have you ever seen so many pipes? And look at the microscope over there.
Tarek: Oh yes, Sherlock Holmes used a microscope to solve his cases. He looked at blood and fingerprints and that was new in the 19th century.
Lily: Huh, who's that?
Tarek: Oh, that's a wax model of Dr Watson, Sherlock Holmes's friend.
Ava: Look, there's Sherlock Holmes, too.
Harry: Oh, and here's his bedroom. It looks so real, it's hard to believe that Sherlock Holmes didn't live here.
Ava: Yes, look, they've left a newspaper on his desk.
Lily: And a book next to his bed.
Harry: They've also put his violin next to his desk.
Tarek: I wonder what's up there? Oh wow! Guys, come up here. This is really funny. I've found Sherlock Holmes's toilet!

6b

Make a list of things you can see at the museum.
Liste die Dinge auf, die man im Museum sehen kann.

At the Sherlock Holmes Museum you can see:

many pipes, a ______________________________

____

____

6c

Work in groups of four. Choose a role: Lily, Harry, Tarek or Ava. Listen to the dialogue again and read along. Practise your role and act out the dialogue.
Arbeitet in Vierergruppen. Wählt eine Rolle aus: Lily, Harry, Tarek oder Ava. Hört euch den Dialog noch einmal an und lest mit. Übt eure Rolle und spielt den Dialog vor.

Museums in London

7a

Look at the photos. What can you see? Match the words to the photos. There are two more words than you need. Sieh dir die Fotos an. Was kannst du sehen? Ordne die Wörter den Fotos zu. Es gibt zwei Wörter mehr als du brauchst.

1

2

rocket | walrus | old coins | buses | space capsule | taxi

3

4

7b

Read the texts about the museums and look at the photos. Which text goes with which photo? Lies die Texte über die Museen und sieh dir die Fotos an. Welcher Text passt zu welchem Foto?

Text A goes with photo number ...

A ☐	At the **Science Museum** you can see and touch objects like clocks, telephones, planes or this Apollo 10 space capsule.
B ☐	The **Horniman Museum** has many different collections of instruments. The most famous object in the museum is an overstuffed walrus.
C ☐	At the **London Transport Museum** you can find every type of vehicle that ever drove on London's streets.
D ☐	At the **Museum of London** you can learn about the history of London. There are Roman coins from 2,000 years ago.

LAND & LEUTE 7 video 13

Museen in London

In London gibt es über 200 unterschiedliche Museen – vom *Arsenal Football Club Museum* bis zum *Wimbledon Windmill Museum*. Drei der beliebtesten Museen finden sich in unmittelbarer Nachbarschaft zueinander in Kensington: Das *Science Museum*, das *Natural History Museum* und das *Victoria and Albert Museum (V&A)*.

Im *Science Museum* kannst du die wichtigsten technischen Entwicklungen der letzten 300 Jahre sehen, anfassen und zum Teil auch ausprobieren. Gleich nebenan, im *Natural History Museum*, steht ein lebensgroßes Modell eines T-Rex.
Im *V&A* gibt es eine fantastische Sammlung der Mode der letzten Jahrhunderte.

Gibt es bei dir in der Nähe ähnliche Angebote?

Announcements

8

audio 34

Listen to the announcements and circle the right answers.
Höre dir die Durchsagen an und kreise die richtigen Antworten ein.

1 Wann schließt das Museum? ***14.30 h / 15.30 h***

2 Warum ist die Ägypten-Ausstellung heute nicht geöffnet?
Das Licht / Der Lautsprecher *ist kaputt.*

3 Was darf man im Museum nicht? ***Musik hören / Fotos machen***

4 Worum wird in der 4. Ansage gebeten? *Um* ***Geldspenden / Videoclips***

5 Was trägt das Mädchen, das verloren gegangen ist?
Ein ***gelbes / rosa*** *T-Shirt und weiße Shorts*

6 Wie heißen die Gemälde von Picasso? *Die drei* ***Fischer / Tänzer***

A museum of everyday objects

9

audio 35

Listen to the children after their visit to the Sherlock Holmes Museum. What is Lily's idea? Tick. ✓ Höre den Kindern nach ihrem Besuch im Sherlock Holmes Museum zu. Was ist Lilys Idee? Mache ein Häkchen.

Lily would like to make an exhibition out of her

☐ socks. ☐ room. ☐ board games.

Museums

10

Write quiz cards for your classmates like these. Think of more. Schreibe Quizkarten für deine Mitschüler / Mitschülerinnen wie diese. Denke dir weitere aus.

A *You can see a collection of pipes and a violin here. Which museum is it?*

1 The Sherlock Holmes Museum
2 The British Museum
3 The Museum of London

B *What can you see at the London Transport Museum?*

A red ______________________
____

C *Where can you see old coins?*

At the ______________________
____

Have you ever …?

11a

audio 36

Listen to the song and sing along. Höre dir das Lied an und sing mit.

Have you ever been to Paris?
Have you ever been to Rome?
Have you ever been to London?
No, I've just been here at home.

Have you ever met a stunt man?
Have you ever met the Queen?
Have you ever met a T-Rex?
No, I've just seen them on screen.

Have you ever eaten snails?
Have you ever eaten snake?
Have you ever eaten frogs' legs?
No, I've just had too much cake.

Have you ever done a back flip?
Have you ever done things wrong?
Have you ever done a marathon?
No, I've just done a song and the last line got too long.

11b

Write down five questions in your exercise book. Work with a partner. Ask and answer questions. Take turns. Schreibe fünf Fragen in dein Heft. Arbeitet zu zweit. Stellt Fragen und beantwortet sie. Wechselt einander ab.

Have you ever	been to	Paris?
	visited	to a museum?
	met	the Queen?
	eaten	snakes?
	seen	a mummy?
	touched	London?
		a walrus?

Yes, I have.

No, I haven't.

We proudly present

12a

Take a look at the friends' exhibition of everyday things and match them to the texts. **Sieh dir die Ausstellung von Alltagsgegenständen der Freunde an und ordne sie den Texten zu.**

1

2

3

4

A	This beautiful vase is Grandma Edyta's masterpiece. You can see two painted roses on the vase. It is 40cm tall and weighs 2.3kg.
B	Lily designed this lamp when she still lived in Brighton. She used aluminium and plastic. The modern design makes it special. It is 38cm tall and weighs 1.3kg.
C	These pink trainers play an important role in Mrs Kogan's life. She wore these trainers when she ran her first marathon in 2013. Mrs Kogan is a great athlete now and has run many marathons since 2019. The trainers are size six and weigh 280g.
D	This is Harry's first guitar. It is a wooden guitar for children. Harry played this instrument when he was five years old. The guitar is green. It is 62cm long and weighs 510g.

12b

Read the texts again and underline three pieces of information each.
Lies die Texte noch einmal und unterstreiche jeweils drei Informationen.

12c

Have you got a special object? Talk about it in a small group.
Habt ihr einen besonderen Gegenstand? Sprecht in einer Kleingruppe darüber.

My ... is special to me because ...

I got it from ... · ... is old and ... · ... is my favourite colour. · ... I like its colour / size / material. · ...

The great opening

13a

What have the friends done? Match ⌐ the sentence parts. Write the sentences in your exercise book. Was haben die Freunde gemacht? Ordne die Satzteile einander zu. Schreibe die Sätze in dein Heft.

They have tidied	everyday objects.
They have cleaned	a brochure.
They have collected	their parents for special things.
They have asked	the room.
They have written	old tables.

13b

What has Lily forgotten?
Was hat Lily vergessen?

Lily has forgotten to

☐ talk to Ellen. ☐ close the rabbit cage. ☐ clean her room.

Describing objects

14

Read the text and fill in the gaps. Lies den Text und fülle die Lücken aus.

cycle · small · blue · first · old · lot

This b__ __ __ __ children's bike was Gina's f__ __ __ __ __ bike.

It is now ten years o__ __ __ and much too s__ __ __ __ __ for her.

Gina liked her bike a l__ __ __ .

She used it to c__ __ __ __ __ up and down the street.

Our exhibition of everyday objects TARGET TASK

15 media worksheet C

Write a short text about an everyday object. Follow the steps. Schreibe einen kurzen Text über einen Alltagsgegenstand. Folge den Arbeitsschritten.

Step 1

What would you show in an exhibition of everyday objects? Was würdest du in einer Ausstellung von Alltagsgegenständen zeigen?

Think about: Denke nach über:

things you can find at school / things you have at home / things you have created

Step 2

Write a text. Schreibe einen Text.

How can you describe your object? Wie kannst du dein Objekt beschreiben?
(colour: red, blue, green …
size: small, big, long, short …
material: plastic, wood, paper …)

How old is your object?
Wie alt ist dein Objekt?
(… years old, … my first …,
I got it when I was … years old)

What do (did) you do with it?
Was mach(te)st du damit?
(I play / played with it.
I cycle / cycled …
I take / took it with me to …)

Where is it from?
(My mum / dad / … gave it to me.
It was a Christmas / birthday present.
It is from a holiday in Poland / Spain / …
I bought it with my first pocket money.)

Step 3

Display your texts in class. Stellt eure Texte in der Klasse aus.

Step 4

You can put all your texts together in an exhibition catalogue. If you like, you can organize a real exhibition in your classroom.

Ihr könnte alle eure Text in einem Ausstellungskatalog zusammenstellen. Wenn ihr wollt, könnt ihr eine echte Ausstellung in eurem Klassenzimmer organisieren.

What's on in the holidays?

1a

Read about the holiday activities at the Notting Hill youth club. Match the pictures to the workshops. Lies über die Ferienaktivitäten des Notting Hill Jugendclubs. Verbinde die Bilder mit den Workshops.

NOTTING HILL YOUTH CLUB * HOLIDAY PROGRAMME

For further information on all courses visit ***www.chasgcfv.co.uk***

DRAMA, BABY!
In this one-week drama workshop we're going to write our own version of "The Canterville Ghost" and perform it

KICK IT!
A two-week football practice course with professional coaches

IS IT RUBBISH OR IS IT ART?
Don't throw it away!
We're going to use your old stuff to create beautiful new things in our two-day upcycling workshop

1

2

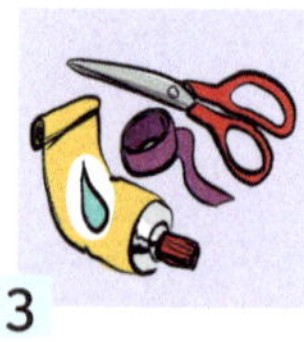
3

1b

Read the notes again. Which workshop would you choose? Say why.
Lies die Notizen erneut. Welchen Workshop würdest du wählen? Sage, warum.

I would choose ______________________________ because I like sports / acting / playing in a team / making things / …

The children's plans

2a audio 37

Listen and read along. What are the children talking about? Höre zu und lies mit. Worüber sprechen die Kinder?

☐ Favourite food ☐ Plans for the holidays

Ava: Have you already got plans for the summer holidays?
Lily: Oh yes, I have. I'm going to join an upcycling workshop at the youth club. I'm really looking forward to creating new things out of old stuff. I'm going to create a new lamp for my room. What are you going to do, Ava?
Ava: We are going to visit my grandmother in Poland for the first two weeks. What about you, Tarek? Are you going to do another cooking workshop?

Tarek: No, I'm not. I thought about the hockey camp, but then I looked at the noticeboard at the youth club. Now I'm going to do a drama workshop there.
Harry: Really? How cool! Are you going to be on stage in a real theatre?
Tarek: Oh yes! There's going to be a performance at the end of the workshop! Why don't you join the workshop, too, Harry?
Harry: I don't know ... Is there going to be music? I'm better at singing than at acting.
Tarek: We're going to create a new version of "The Canterville Ghost". We also need people for lighting, sound, props, costumes, ...
Lily: And Ava and I are going to come and watch your performance! You have to save tickets for us.

2b

Who is going to do what in the summer holidays? Complete the sentences.
Wer macht was in den Sommerferien? Vervollständige die Sätze.

1 Lily is going to ______________________________

2 Ava is going to ______________________________

3 Harry and Tarek are going to ______________________________

do a drama workshop. · join an upcycling workshop. · visit her grandmother.

Your plans

3

What are your plans for the summer holidays? Walk around the classroom and ask each other. **Welche Pläne habt ihr für die Sommerferien? Geht im Klassenzimmer herum und fragt euch gegenseitig.**

Yes, I am.

No, I'm not.

I don't know.

	Name: ____________	Name: ____________	Name: ____________
Are you going to visit your family?			
Are you going to play computer games?			
Are you going to meet friends?			
Are you going to ____________?			

GRAMMAR HELP

Wenn du über Pläne für die Zukunft sprechen möchtest, kannst du das *going to-future* verwenden. Sieh dir die Beispiele an. Was fällt dir auf?

I **am going to** do a drama workshop.
Ava **is going to** go to Poland.
The children **are going to** act in a play.

I **am not going to** do a cooking workshop.
Ava **is not going to** go to Scotland.
The children **are not going to** act in a musical.

Next weekend

4

Write the sentences in the boxes. **Schreibe die Sätze in die Kästen.**

1 Ben is not going to go to London. Ben is going to go to Paris.
2 Jacob is going to sleep in late. Jacob is not going to get up early.
3 Israh and Melike are not going to play football. They are going to go on a bike tour.

going to	not going to

Lots of questions

5

Match the questions and the answers. **Verbinde die Frage und die Antworten.**

1 What is Lily going to do in her workshop?	Harry is not going to act.
2 When are Ava and her family going to go to Poland?	Tarek is going to act in a play.
3 Who is going to act in a play?	They are going to go in the first weeks of the holidays.
4 Why is Harry not going to be on stage?	She is going to create new things out of old stuff.

Try something new, Harry!

7a

Look at the picture. What do you think Tarek is telling Harry?
Sieh dir das Bild an. Was erzählt Tarek Harry wohl?

☐ Tarek is telling Harry about the book. ☐ Tarek is telling Harry about breakfast.

7b audio 38

Listen to Harry and Tarek. What is the ghost's problem in the story?
Höre Harry und Tarek zu. Was ist das Problem des Geists in der Geschichte?

☐ He is lonely. ☐ He is hungry. ☐ He is not scary.

7c audio 38

Listen again and complete the sentences.
Höre noch einmal zu und vervollständige die Sätze.

1 The Canterville ghost lives ____________________

2 One day a family moves ____________________

3 The ghost tries ____________________

4 No one in the family is ____________________

in a very old house · into the house · afraid of the ghost · to scare them away

An email to Gus

8 media worksheet G

Read Harry's email to Gus, the workshop leader, and fill in the gaps with words from the box. Lies Harrys E-Mail an Gus, den Leiter des Workshops, und fülle die Lücken mit Wörtern aus dem Kasten.

workshop · yesterday · friend · join

Dear Gus,

I am Tarek Adil's ____________, Harry. Tarek told me about the drama ____________ in the summer holidays. The deadline to sign up was ____________, but I would really like to take part in the workshop. Can I still ____________?

Yours sincerely, Harry Norris

Get creative

Sieh bei 1a auf S. 114 nach, wenn du Hilfe brauchst. !

9

Create a flyer for a workshop you would like to do in your summer holidays.
Gestalte ein Flugblatt für einen Workshop, den du in den Sommerferien gerne machen würdest.

Title: ______________________________ (Schreibe hier, wie dein Workshop heißen soll.)

We are going to ____

____

______________________________ (Schreibe hier, was du in dem Workshop tun willst.)

Place: ______________________________ (Schreibe hier, wo der Workshop stattfindet.)

Picture: (Zeichne hier ein Bild, das mit deinem Workshop zu tun hat.)

LAND & LEUTE 8 video 14

Theater für Kinder

In London gibt es viele Theater-Angebote, auch speziell für Kinder und Jugendliche. Das Theater *The Unicorn* zum Beispiel bietet Theaterstücke für Kinder in jedem Alter an. Selbst Babys haben hier die Möglichkeit, erste Erfahrungen mit Theater zu machen. Besonders Märchen von den Gebrüdern Grimm oder fantastische Geschichten, wie die von Gullivers Reisen, werden dort gezeigt.

Im *Polka Theatre* in Wimbledon kann man nicht nur Aufführungen anschauen, hier gibt es auch Workshops, an denen die ganze Familie teilnehmen kann. Sogar im berühmten *Globe Theatre*, wo hauptsächlich Stücke von William Shakespeare aufgeführt werden, gibt es besondere Veranstaltungen und Angebote für Kinder.

Zur Weihnachtszeit ist es eine englische Tradition, sich eine *pantomime* anzuschauen. Das hat nichts mit dem deutschen Wort Pantomime (stumme Vorführung) zu tun, sondern ist eine Mischung aus Theater, Musical, Märchen und Comedy. Alle im Publikum sind aufgefordert, aktiv mitzumachen und die Lieder mitzusingen, bei Zaubertricks zu assistieren, den Bösewicht auszubuhen und dem Helden zu helfen, indem sie ihn laut vor Gefahren warnen.

Sieh dir das Video an. Welches Theater in London würdest du gerne besuchen?

At the workshop

11

Read the story. What are the children's ideas for their own version?

Lies die Geschichte. Was sind die Ideen der Kinder für ihre eigene Version?

The Canterville Ghost

12a audio 39

Listen to the performance at the youth club and read along.
Höre dir die Vorführung im Jugendclub an und lies mit.

SCENE 1: In front of the house *The Otis family arrives at Canterville House.*
Mrs Otis: This is our new home.
The twins: Ohhh! Is there a ghost here?
Mr Otis: No. Ghosts don't exist.
Sir Simon: What? I don't exist? I'll show these people how scary I am.

SCENE 2: In the twins' bedroom
Sir Simon: *(rattles his chains)* Aahhh! I am the ghost of Sir Simon de Canterville. This is my house. Go away!
David: *(tired)* What's all this noise? We want to sleep!
Jack: *(bored)* Go away, Mr Ghost. We're tired.

SCENE 3: In Mr and Mrs Otis' bedroom *(sound)* CLANG, CLANG, CLANG
Sir Simon: *(loud)* Wake up! I am the ghost of Canterville House!
Mrs Otis: Excuse me, Mr Ghost, please stop making all that noise.
Mr Otis: We can't sleep.
Sir Simon: *(frustrated)* It's impossible to live in the same house as this family!

SCENE 4: On the stairs *(sound)* CLONK, CLONK, CLONK
Sir Simon: I'm going to frighten everybody. I must practise my terrible laughter. Haaa. Haaaa. Haaa.
Mr Otis: What's all this about?
David: Go away!
Jack: And let us sleep.
Sir Simon: Haaaa! My terrible laughter will ... *(falls down the stairs)* CRASH!
Otis family: Hahaha!

SCENE 5: In the living room
Sir Simon: *(sad)* I'm not a good ghost.
Mrs Otis: Why are you crying?
Sir Simon: I'm sad. I can't stay if you're not afraid of me. The ghost inspector will find out, and I will have to leave.
Mr Otis: Don't worry. We'll help you. Where are the twins?

SCENE 6: Somewhere in the house *The ghost inspector has arrived.*
Sir Simon: *(rattles his chains)* BOO!
David and Jack: *(run away)* Aaaah!
Sir Simon: *(shows his terrible laughter)* Haaa. Haaaa. Haaa.
Mrs and Mrs Otis: Help!
Ghost inspector: Well done, Sir Simon. Very scary. You may stay at Canterville House. Goodbye.
David: Is he gone?
Sir Simon: Yes, I think he's gone.
The family and Sir Simon: Yipppeeeee!

12b

Read the script again. Then match the questions and the answers.
Lies das Skript noch einmal. Verbinde dann die Fragen und die Antworten.

1 What does Mr Otis say about ghosts?	He feels very sad and starts crying.
2 Who are the twins?	No, he can't.
3 Who is Sir Simon?	He says they don't exist.
4 Can Sir Simon scare the Otis family?	He is the ghost of Canterville House.
5 How does Sir Simon feel then?	They help Sir Simon with the ghost inspector.
6 What does the Otis family do for Sir Simon?	They are the sons of Mr and Mrs Otis.

12c

Work in groups. Choose one scene from the play and do a dramatic reading.
Arbeitet in Gruppen. Sucht euch eine Szene des Theaterstücks aus und macht eine dramatische Lesung.

Ghostly questions

13

A German ghost has questions about Sir Simon. Look at the script again and answer them in German. Ein deutscher Geist hat Fragen über Sir Simon. Lies das Skript noch einmal und beantworte sie auf Deutsch.

1 Wie versucht Sir Simon, die Familie zu erschrecken?

Er ______________________________

2 Warum kommt da ein Inspektor?

____

3 Wie geht das aus?

____

Drama words

14

Unscramble the words and write them down.
Entwirre die Wörter und schreibe sie auf.

1 rloe r ______
2 atcor a ______
3 sence s ______
4 pecnefromra p ______

Improve your performance

15

Match the German and the English sentences.
Ordne die deutschen und die englischen Sätze einander zu.

1 Sprich laut und deutlich.	Practise in your group.
2 Lerne deinen Text auswendig.	Learn your text by heart.
3 Übe in deiner Gruppe.	Speak loudly and clearly.

Words and moods

16a

Match the English and the German adjectives.
Ordne die englischen und die deutschen Adjektive einander zu.

sad | angry | excited | bored | happy | scared | worried | tired

aufgeregt | traurig | wütend | glücklich | gelangweilt | müde | besorgt | verängstigt

16b

Work with a partner. Say each sentence in a different mood. Your partner has to guess the mood. **Arbeitet zu zweit. Sagt jeden Satz in einer anderen Stimmung. Dein Partner / Deine Partnerin muss die Stimmung erraten.**

1 Ohhh! Is there a ghost here?
2 What's all this about?
3 What? I don't exist?
4 Yes, I think he's gone.
5 I'll have to be even scarier tomorrow.
6 Go away!

Our play TARGET TASK

17

Perform a scene from *The Canterville Ghost*.
Stelle eine Szene aus *The Canterville Ghost* dar.

Step 1

Work in small groups. Choose one scene.
Arbeitet in Kleingruppen. Wählt eine Szene aus.

Step 2

Choose your roles. Wählt eure Rollen.

Step 3

Write down what your character says and learn it by heart.
Schreibe auf, was deine Figur sagt, und lerne es auswendig.

Step 4

Write cue cards with some of the words to help you remember, but don't write the whole text on the cue cards!
Schreibe Stichwortkarten mit ein paar der Wörter, um dir zu helfen, dich zu erinnern, aber schreibe nicht den ganzen Text auf die Stichwortkarten!

Step 5

Sit in a circle and practise reading.
Setzt euch in einen Kreis und übt zu lesen.

Step 6

Present your scene. Präsentiert eure Szene.

Verb forms

1

Look at the verbs and number the matching verb forms.
Sieh dir die Verben an und nummeriere die passenden Verbformen.

1 be | 2 clean | 3 do | 4 eat | 5 find | 6 meet | 7 see | 8 touch | 9 visit | 10 write

☐ seen | ☐ written | ☐ eaten | ☐ done | ☐ met

☐ touched | 1 been | ☐ visited | ☐ found | ☐ cleaned

Quiz

2

Read the texts and match them to the objects. There is one more object than you need. **Lies die Texte und ordne sie den Gegenständen zu. Es gibt einen Gegenstand mehr als du brauchst.**

A My object is grey. It's made of metal. I use it when it's dark. I had to change the batteries four times. My Grandpa gave it to me for my 5th birthday.

B This object is green and has lots of flowers on it. It has a key to open it. I put my money into it. I always keep it on my bookshelf. I got it from Aunt Mary.

teddy bear

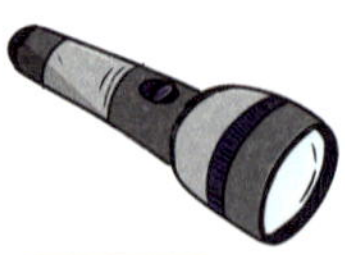
torch

rucksack

piggy bank

knife

C My object is soft and cuddly. It always sat on my bed when I was small. Mum gave it to me when I was a baby. I still love it.

D Dad gave it to me for my camping trip to Scotland. It is made of metal. I used it to cut bread.

What are they going to do?

Write what the people are going to do and what they are not going to do.
Schreibe, was die Leute tun werden und was sie nicht tun werden.

John: (–) fly to Australia / (+) go camping *John is not going to fly to Australia.*

He is going to go camping.

Sally: (–) read a book / (+) watch TV

Joanna and Rick: (–) play a game / (+) meet friends

Mum and Dad: (–) go out for dinner / (+) have a picnic

Who says what?

Read the sentences. Write them into the right boxes.
Lies die Sätze. Schreibe sie in die richtigen Kästen.

Ghosts don't exist. · We want to sleep! · We'll help you. · I'm going to frighten everybody in this family. · Why are you crying? · What's all this noise? · You may stay at Canterville House.

Sir Simon	Mr Otis

Mrs Otis	David and Jack (the twins)	ghost inspector

Important words

Was man in den Ferien machen kann:

play football,

Wörter zum Beschreiben eines Gegenstandes:

long,

Wörter, die ich mir merken möchte:

Numbers

0 oh, zero, nil /əʊ, ˈzɪərəʊ, nɪl/
1 one /wʌn/
2 two /tuː/
3 three /θriː/
4 four /fɔː/
5 five /faɪv/
6 six /sɪks/
7 seven /sevn/
8 eight /eɪt/
9 nine /naɪn/
10 ten /ten/
11 eleven /ɪˈlevn/
12 twelve /twelv/
13 **thir**teen /ˌθɜːˈtiːn/
14 fourteen /ˌfɔːˈtiːn
15 **fif**teen /ˌfɪfˈtiːn/
16 sixteen /ˌsɪksˈtiːn/
17 seventeen /ˌsevnˈtiːn/
18 **eigh**teen /ˌeɪˈtiːn/
19 nineteen /ˌnaɪnˈtiːn/
20 **twen**ty /ˈtwenti/

21 twenty-one /ˌtwentiˈwʌn/
30 **thir**ty /ˈθɜːti/
32 thirty-two /ˌθɜːtiˈtuː/
40 **for**ty /ˈfɔːti/
43 forty-three /ˌfɔːtiˈθriː/
50 **fif**ty /ˈfɪfti/
54 fifty-four /ˌfɪftiˈfɔː/
60 sixty /ˈsɪksti/
65 sixty-five /ˌsɪkstiˈfaɪv/
70 seventy /ˈsevnti/
76 seventy-six /ˌsevntiˈsɪks/
80 **eigh**ty /ˈeɪti/
87 eighty-seven /ˌeɪtiˈsevn/
90 ninety /ˈnaɪnti/
98 ninety-eight /ˌnaɪntiˈeɪt/

100 a/one hundred /ə/wʌn ˈhʌndrəd/
101 one hundred and one /wʌn ˌhʌndrəd‿ən ˈwʌn/
200 two hundred /tuː ˈhʌndrəd/

1,000 one thousand /ə/wʌn ˈθaʊznd/
2,000 two thousand /tuː ˈθaʊznd/

1st **first** /fɜːst/
2nd **second** /ˈsekənd/
3rd **third** /θɜːd/
4th fourth /fɔːθ/
5th **fif**th /fɪfθ/
6th sixth /sɪksθ/
7th seventh /sevnθ/
8th **eigh**th /eɪtθ/
9th **nin**th /naɪnθ/
10th tenth /tenθ/
11th eleventh /ɪˈlevnθ/
12th **twelf**th /twelfθ/

$\frac{1}{2}$ a / one half /ə/wʌn ˈhɑːf/
$\frac{1}{3}$ a / one third /ə/wʌn ˈθɜːd/
$\frac{1}{4}$ a / one quarter /ə/wʌn ˈkwɔːtə/
$\frac{1}{8}$ a / one eighth /ə/wʌn‿ˈeɪtθ/
$\frac{3}{4}$ three quarters /θriː ˈkwɔːtəz/

!
Daten schreibst du so:
1 August, 2 January, 5 November
oder so:
1st August, 2nd January, 5th November

Holidays

DIGITAL+ video 15

You can travel by ...

bike

boat

bus

car

plane

You can visit ...

a castle

a museum

a zoo

a city

the seaside / a beach

a market

a shopping centre

a church

The weather can be ...

sunny

rainy

cold

warm – hot –
bad – terrible –
good – fantastic –
OK – great – perfect

Places can be ...

new old

big

small

boring ↔ interesting
quiet ↔ loud
good ↔ bad

What do you like doing in your holidays?

I like going sightseeing.

I like doing sports.

Talking about your last holidays

What did you do in the holidays?

I ...

Did you stay at home?

Yes, I did. / No, I didn't.

Where did you go?

I went to Italy.

England – France – Germany – Scotland – Spain – the USA – Wales

What did you do?

I went sightseeing.

I went to an adventure park.

go sightseeing – do sports – go swimming – go cycling – visit relatives – ...

How was it?

It was great because the castle that we visited was very old.

I loved the food. It was very special and yummy.

Getting around

DIGITAL+ video 16

London sights

Where do you want to go?

I'd love to go to Hyde Park / on the London Eye.

We're going to … tomorrow.

Can we go to a museum, too?

We can also see Buckingham Palace.

Big Ben · the River Thames · Sky Garden · Hyde Park · the Natural History Museum · London Zoo · the London Eye · Westminster Abbey · Trafalgar Square · Wembley Stadium · Covent Garden · Platform 9¾ · the Tower of London · Madame Tussauds · …

Buckingham Palace

the Shard

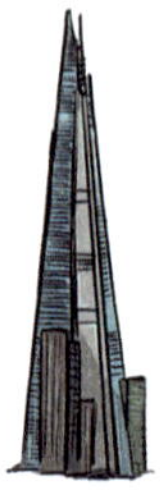

Tower Bridge

Travelling with the Tube

What time does the next train leave?

The next train leaves at 10.48.

Where do we have to change lines?

We change lines at Bond Street and take the Jubilee Line to Westminster Station.

How much are the tickets?

A ticket costs …

Giving or following directions

Turn left!

Turn right!

Walk past …

Go straight on!

Walk on until you get to …

Cross the road!

On your left you can see …

On your right you can see …

Excuse me! How do I get to …?

Turn left here and then walk …

Celebrations

DIGITAL+ video 17

Festivals and holidays around the world

Hogmanay

New Year's Eve

Christmas

Easter · Halloween · Chinese New Year · Diwali · Eid · Bonfire Night · Ramadan · Lantern festival

Religions and cultures

Christians celebrate Christmas and Easter.

Muslims celebrate Eid and Ramadan.

Jewish people celebrate Hanukkah.

Many people around the world celebrate Halloween and New Year's Eve.

Let's celebrate!

We have a meal / a party / ...
We eat snacks / food / ...
We meet relatives / friends / ...
We have fireworks / a bonfire / an Easter egg hunt / music / fun / ...
We play games.
We dress up in costumes.
We light candles.
We dance / sing / ...

Traditions

People in Spain eat 12 grapes at midnight to bring luck for the **new year**.

Jewish people light a candle on the **Hanukkah** menorah for eight days during Hanukkah.

During **Ramadan**, families go to the mosque for a special prayer.

For the **Chinese New Year**, many people clean their houses.

People have bonfires and fireworks to celebrate **Bonfire Night** in the UK.

On **Easter Sunday**, many children look for Easter eggs. In the UK, there are often Easter egg rolls.

Children dress up and knock on doors to ask for sweets at **Halloween**. This is called trick-or-treating.

Rules

You must ... / You mustn't ...

You must wear school uniform.

You must do your homework.

You must not run in school.

You mustn't eat in the classroom.

You must always listen to the teacher.

You must show respect and be quiet.

You mustn't listen to music in the classroom.

You mustn't use your mobile phone in class.

Following the rules

We can drink during lessons, but we can't eat in the classroom.

We are allowed to bring our mobile phones to school, but we aren't allowed to use them in class.

We have to wear school uniform.

We must be on time.

We must not wear make-up.

We don't have to carry our school books around with us.

Asking for something

Can I watch TV now? – Yes, you can. / No, you can't.
Am I allowed to have some sweets? – Yes, you are. / No, you aren't.
May I go to the cinema with my friends? – Yes, you may. / No, you may not.

Talking about conflicts

Problems

You play on your computer too much.

You go to bed too late.

You watch too much TV.

You haven't tidied your room.

You stayed out too late with your friends at the party on Saturday.

Arguments

Can I go to the park to play football with my friends?

No, you have to do your homework first.

Fine. You can go, but you have to be home by 6pm!

Thank you very much!

Why don't we go to the party?

I'm tired, I would rather watch a film.

Please let's go!

Why don't you go alone? Then we can both do what we want!

Good idea!

Discussions

I want to … · I don't want to … · I would like to … · Why can't I …? · Could we …? · All my friends are allowed to … · OK then. · Sorry. · What about …? · That's a good idea. ·

I feel …

angry · annoyed · bad · bored · excited · frustrated · good · happy · relaxed · sad · scared · terrible · tired · worried

Wildlife

DIGITAL+ video 18

Nature

trees · flowers ·
animals · forest ·
mountain · beach ·
grass · leaves ·

Things to do in nature

horse riding · cycling ·
watching animals · swimming ·
walking your dog ·
going for walks · ...

Where can we find wild animals?

at a national park / forest / zoo / garden / park / beach · in the street

Protecting the environment

We need to protect the environment.

Excellent. Let's make a list.

We can build a bee hotel.

We can leave parts of the garden with long grass.

Perfect. Let's go.

Wild animals

squirrel

bird

turtle

dolphin

insects

bee

tortoise

hedgehog

fox

mouse

Jobs

DIGITAL+ video 19

Who does what?

A firefighter fights fires.

A photographer takes pictures with a camera.

A chef cooks food for people.

A pilot flies planes.

A police officer helps people in trouble.

A singer sings on a stage.

A hairdresser cuts people's hair.

A vet helps sick animals.

Talking about the future

DIGITAL+ video 20

When I grow up ...

I'll be a really famous singer. I'll play the world's biggest stages.

When I'm older, I want to be an engineer. I'll invent lots of useful things.

When I grow up, I'll be a famous fashion designer.

When I grow up, I'll be a chef and have my own restaurant.

Making plans

In the summer holidays, I'm going to do a drama workshop!

I am going to practise acting.

There is going to be a performance at the end of the workshop.

Describing people

People can be ...

careful · slow · fast ·
beautiful · funny ·
good · bad · quiet · nice ·
young · old ·
cool · friendly ·
clever · stupid ·
famous · loud ·
short · tall

He is feeling excited.
He is jumping excitedly.

People can feel ...

happy · sad ·
worried · sick ·
terrible · bored ·
scared · surprised ·
calm · angry ·
excited

They are angry.
They are shouting angrily.

Adjectives and adverbs

careful	→	carefully
slow	→	slowly
loud	→	loudly
fast	→	**fast**
happy	→	happ**ily**
good	→	**well**
beautiful	→	beautifully
calm	→	calmly

They did really well.

She is a careful person.
She rides her bike carefully.

Good style

Every text needs …

- a beginning
- a middle
- an ending

What else should your text have?

- an interesting title
- a good first sentence
- adjectives, adverbs and linking words

first / at the beginning → then → after that → finally / in the end

Plan your story

Who? → my friend John
Where? → the moon
When? → 2062
What? → time travelling

Linking words

and · or · but · because · so · so that · before · when

She has to go shopping **so that** she can eat.

She wanted to eat, **but** the food didn't taste good. The food didn't taste good, **so** she didn't eat it.

They discuss what to do **when** it is raining outside.

He always brushes his teeth **before** he goes to bed.

Students and teachers are outside **and** walk around **or** talk.

Noah has to go home **because** it is late.

1 So kannst du sagen, was (gestern, letzte Woche oder letztes Jahr) passiert ist:

a) Regelmäßige Verben: Du hängst **-ed** an die Grundform:

They watch**ed** a film yesterday.
We visit**ed** Wales last summer.

b) Unregelmäßige Verben musst du lernen.
Sie sind in der Vokabelliste mit *(irr)* gekennzeichnet. Du findest sie in der zweiten Spalte der Tabelle auf den Seiten 146 und 147.

They **had** a great holiday.
Tarek **went** to Wales with his father.

c) Das Verb *be* hat als einziges Verb zwei Formen in der Vergangenheit:

She **was** in Scotland **last weekend**.
They **were** in London **last summer**.

2 So kannst du sagen, was (gestern, letzte Woche oder letztes Jahr) nicht passiert ist:

Du verneinst regelmäßige und unregelmäßige Verben mit **didn't (= did not)** und fügst die Grundform des Verbs hinzu:

They **didn't** watch a video clip yesterday.
We **didn't** visit England last summer.
She **didn't** have a bad holiday.
Tarek **didn't** go to Scotland with his father.

Bei *was* und *were* hängst du ***not*** oder die Kurzform ***n't*** an:

She **wasn't** in Paris **last weekend**.
We **weren't** in England **last summer**.

3 So kannst du fragen, was (gestern, letzte Woche oder letztes Jahr) passiert ist:

Did they watch a film?	Yes, they did. / No, they didn't.
Did Tarek visit Wales?	Yes, he did. / No, he didn't.
Was she in London last weekend?	Yes, she was. / No, she wasn't.
Were you in Scotland last summer?	Yes, we were. / No, we weren't.
How was your holiday?	It was ...
What did you do?	I did ... / played ... / visited ...
Where did you go?	I went to ...

4 So vergleichst du Personen oder Dinge:

a) Einsilbige Adjektive: Du hängst **-er** oder **-est** an.

I think the park is nice.
Yes, but I think the zoo is nic**er**.
But London Eye is the nic**est**.

b) Mehrsilbige Adjektive:
Du stellst **more** oder **most** vor das Adjektiv.

I think the park is interesting.
Yes, but I think the zoo is **more** interesting.
But London Eye is the **most** interesting.

c) Vergleichssätze: Sind Personen oder Dinge, die du vergleichst, unterschiedlich, verwendest du **than** und die Form mit *-er* oder *more*. Sind sie gleich, verwendest du **as ... as** mit der Grundform des Adjektivs.

Ava is older **than** Joshua.
Lily is **as** old **as** Harry.

5 So kannst du über etwas sprechen, das jemand regelmäßig macht oder das allgemein gültig ist:

He **plays** the guitar. He **doesn't play** the piano.

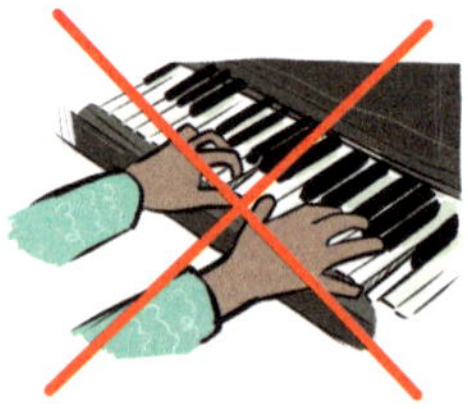

They **love** dancing.

The boy **doesn't** play football.

I **don't** like tests.

6 So stellst du Fragen:

Does Ollie **like** carrots?
Do you **live** in London?
Where **do** you **live**?
What do the children play?
When can the children go to the park?
What have the children got in their bags?
When is your birthday?

7 So sagst du, was jemand gerade tut:

Noah **is brushing** his teeth.
He **isn't taking** a shower.

The girls **are playing** basketball.
They **aren't playing** football.

8 So fragst du, was jemand gerade tut:

Is the man **loading** the dishwasher?
Yes, he is.

Are the children **playing** football?
No, they aren't.

9 So sagst du, ob du viel oder nicht viel von etwas hast:

a) Die Mengenangaben *some* und *any*:

There are **some** tomatoes in the fridge.
Are there **any** apples? No, there aren't.
I need **some** milk for my cornflakes.
Have you got **any** milk?
We have**n't** got **any** milk.

b) Die Mengenangaben *much*, *many* und *a lot of*:

Much verwendest du mit Nomen, die nicht zählbar sind.
Many verwendest du mit zählbaren Nomen.
Beide Wörter verwendest du meist in verneinten Aussagesätzen oder Fragen.

We haven't got **much** milk.
How **much** money have we got?
We haven't got **many** tomatoes.
How **many** tomatoes have we got?

A lot of oder *lots of* verwendest du meist in bejahten Aussagesätzen. Es spielt keine Rolle, ob die Nomen zählbar oder nicht zählbar sind.

We need **lots of** milk. We need **a lot of** orange juice.
We need **lots of** tomatoes. We need **a lot of** apples.

10 So sagst du, was jemand tun muss oder nicht tun darf:

Students **must** wear school uniform.
Students **have to** wear school uniform.
Tarek **has to** wear a tie.

The boy **mustn't** run in the school building.

11 So sagst du, was erlaubt oder nicht erlaubt ist:

Students **can** bring their mobiles to school, but they **can't** use them.

Students **are allowed to** bring their mobiles to school, but they **aren't allowed to** use them.

Why **are** they **not allowed** to use them?

Dad, **can** I go to the party on Saturday?

Usually I'm allowed to stay out until eight o'clock, but today I can stay out until nine.

Dad, **am I allowed to** go to the party on Saturday?

Students **may** use their mobiles at lunchtime in the cafeteria.

They **may not** use them during lessons.

May I open the window, please?

12 So bildest du Sätze im Englischen:

Subjekt, Verb und Objekt stehen in englischen Sätze immer in dieser Reihenfolge:
We meet our friends.

Dann können noch Ergänzungen folgen. Gibt es Ortsangaben und Zeitangaben, nennt man erst den Ort und dann die Zeit.

We meet our friends in the park on Saturdays.

13 So kannst du Vermutungen über die Zukunft ausdrücken oder Vorhersagen machen:

I **will** be famous. (= I**'ll** be famous.)

He **will** have a lot of money.

We **won't** (= **will not**) live in London when we are older.

She **won't** (= **will not**) have a regular job.

14 So kannst du Fragen über die Zukunft stellen:

Will you be a famous fashion designer?	Yes, I **will**. / No, I **won't**.
Will we live in New York?	Yes, we **will**. / No, we **won't**.
Will Harry be rich?	Yes, he **will**. / No, he **won't**.
Where will you live?	We **will** live in ...
What will you do?	I **will** ...

15 So kannst du beschreiben, wie jemand etwas tut:

Du hängst die Endung ***-ly*** an ein Adjektiv, wenn du ein Adverb bilden willst, das beschreibt, **wie** jemand etwas tut:

The band is playing loud**ly**.

Einige Adverbien haben Sonderformen:
good: **well**, fast: **fast**, hard: **hard**

Kate and Jonathan walked down the stairs slowly and carefully.

16 So kannst du Sätze oder Teile eines Satzes miteinander verbinden:

Mr Patel is our English teacher, **and** Mrs Fisher is our PE teacher.	... **und** ...
We could watch a film, **or** we could play a game.	... **oder** ...
I like ice cream, **but** I don't like chocolate.	... **aber** ...
Ava is happy **because** she can play with Ollie now.	... **weil** ...
I smile **when** I see my dog.	... **wenn** ...
We have enough food **so** we don't need to go shopping.	... **also** ...
I know **that** I have to do my homework.	... **dass** ...
The sign is very big **so that** the visitors can see it.	... **sodass** ...
You should wash your hands **before** you eat.	... **bevor** ...

17 So kannst du über etwas sprechen, das vergangen ist, aber noch Einfluss auf die Gegenwart hat:

Du brauchst die Formen ***have*** oder ***has*** und das Partizip Perfekt. Das Partizip Perfekt bildest du, indem du die Endung ***-ed*** an die Grundform des Verbs hängst:

I **have cleaned** the kitchen. I **haven't cleaned** the living room yet.
He **has** just **finished** his homework. He **hasn't walked** the dog.
We **have been** to Paris many times. We **haven't been** to London.

Die Formen der unregelmäßigen Verben – z. B. ***been***, ***done***, ***had*** – musst du auswendig lernen. Du findest sie in der dritten Spalte der Tabelle auf den Seiten 146 und 147.

18 So kannst du fragen, ob jemand schon mal etwas gemacht hat:

Have you ever **been** to London?	Yes, I have. / No, I haven't.
Has Ava **bought** a new book?	Yes, she has. / No, she hasn't.
Have the children **finished** their homework?	Yes, they have. / No, they haven't.
What have you **done**?	
Where have you **been**?	

19 So kannst du über Pläne für die Zukunft sprechen:

I'm **going to** do a drama workshop.

He is **going to** take part in the show.

We are **not going to** do the cooking workshop.

They are**n't going to** act in the play.

I'm going to create a new lamp in the workshop. It's going to be fun!

20 So kannst du fragen, was für Pläne jemand für die Zukunft hat:

Are you **going to** do a cooking workshop?	Yes, I am. / No, I'm not.
Is Ava **going to** visit her grandmother?	Yes, she is. / No, she isn't.
Are the children **going to** act in a play?	Yes, they are. / No, they aren't.
What are you **going to** do in the holidays?	
When is the workshop **going to** start?	

Irregular Verbs

infinitive		simple past		past participle	
be	sein	**was/were**	war/waren	**been**	gewesen
become	werden	**became**	wurde	**become**	geworden
break	brechen	**broke**	brach	**broken**	gebrochen
bring	(mit)bringen	**brought**	brachte (mit)	**brought**	(mit)gebracht
build	bauen	**built**	baute	**built**	gebaut
buy	kaufen	**bought**	kaufte	**bought**	gekauft
choose	wählen; sich entscheiden	**chose**	wählte; entschied sich	**chosen**	gewählt; sich entschieden
come	kommen	**came**	kam	**come**	gekommen
cut	schneiden	**cut**	schnitt	**cut**	geschnitten
do	machen; tun	**did**	machte, tat	**done**	gemacht, getan
draw	zeichnen	**drew**	zeichnete	**drawn**	gezeichnet
drive	fahren	**drove**	fuhr	**driven**	gefahren
eat	essen	**ate**	aß	**eaten**	gegessen
fall down	hinfallen	**fell down**	fiel hin	**fallen down**	hingefallen
feed	füttern	**fed**	fütterte	**fed**	gefüttert
feel	fühlen	**felt**	fühlte	**felt**	gefühlt
fight	kämpfen	**fought**	kämpfte	**fought**	gekämpft
find	finden	**found**	fand	**found**	gefunden
fly	fliegen	**flew**	flog	**flown**	geflogen
get	(be)kommen; werden	**got**	(be)kam; wurde	**got**	bekommen / gekommen, geworden
give	geben	**gave**	gab	**given**	gegeben
go	gehen	**went**	ging	**gone**	gegangen
grow up	erwachsen werden	**grew up**	wurde erwachsen	**grown up**	erwachsen geworden
hang (up)	aufhängen	**hung (up)**	hing auf	**hung (up)**	aufgehängt
have	haben	**had**	hatte	**had**	gehabt
hide	verstecken	**hid**	versteckte	**hidden**	versteckt
keep	behalten, halten	**kept**	behielt, hielt	**kept**	behalten, gehalten
know	kennen, wissen	**knew**	kannte, wusste	**known**	gekannt, gewusst
learn	lernen	**learnt**	lernte	**learnt**	gelernt
leave	zurücklassen; weggehen	**left**	ließ zurück; ging weg	**left**	zurückgelassen; weggegangen
let	lassen	**let**	ließ	**let**	gelassen
light	anzünden	**lit**	zündete an	**lit**	angezündet
make	machen	**made**	machte	**made**	gemacht
meet	treffen	**met**	traf	**met**	getroffen
pay	(be)zahlen	**paid**	(be)zahlte	**paid**	be- / gezahlt
put	setzen, legen, stellen	**put**	setzte, legte, stellte	**put**	gesetzt, gelegt, gestellt

infinitive		simple past		past participle	
read	lesen	**read**	las	**read**	gelesen
ride	fahren; reiten	**rode**	fuhr; ritt	**ridden**	gefahren; geritten
ring	klingeln; läuten	**rang**	klingelte, läutete	**rung**	geklingelt, geläutet
run	laufen, rennen	**ran**	lief, rannte	**run**	gelaufen, gerannt
say	sagen	**said**	sagte	**said**	gesagt
see	sehen	**saw**	sah	**seen**	gesehen
send	schicken	**sent**	schickte	**sent**	geschickt
show	zeigen	**showed**	zeigte	**shown**	gezeigt
sing	singen	**sang**	sang	**sung**	gesungen
sit	sitzen	**sat**	saß	**sat**	gesessen
sleep	schlafen	**slept**	schlief	**slept**	geschlafen
speak	sprechen, reden	**spoke**	sprach, redete	**spoken**	gesprochen, geredet
spend	ausgeben *(Geld)*; verbringen *(Zeit)*	**spent**	gab aus *(Geld)*; verbrachte *(Zeit)*	**spent**	ausgegeben *(Geld)*; verbracht *(Zeit)*
stand	stehen	**stood**	stand	**stood**	gestanden
stick to	sich halten an	**stuck to**	hielt sich an	**stuck to**	sich gehalten an
swim	schwimmen	**swam**	schwamm	**swum**	geschwommen
take	bringen; nehmen	**took**	brachte; nahm	**taken**	gebracht; genommen
tell	erzählen	**told**	erzählte	**told**	erzählt
think	denken; glauben	**thought**	dachte; glaubte	**thought**	gedacht; geglaubt
throw	werfen	**threw**	warf	**thrown**	geworfen
wake up	aufwachen	**woke up**	wachte auf	**woken up**	aufgewacht
wear	tragen *(Kleidung)*	**wore**	trug *(Kleidung)*	**worn**	getragen *(Kleidung)*
write	schreiben	**wrote**	schrieb	**written**	geschrieben

A

a, an	ein(e)
about	über; an
above	über
(to) **go abroad**	ins Ausland fahren
acrobat	(der) Akrobat / (die) Akrobatin
(to) **act**	handeln; spielen
acting	(das) Schauspielern
activity	(die) Aktivität
actor/actress	(der) Schauspieler/ (die) Schauspielerin
(to) **add**	hinzufügen
address	(die) Adresse
adjective	(das) Adjektiv
adult	(der) Erwachsene / (die) Erwachsene
adventure	(das) Abenteuer
adventure park	(der) Erlebnispark
(to) **be afraid of** *(irr)*	Angst haben vor
after	nach
afternoon	(der) Nachmittag
again	wieder; noch einmal
... ago	vor ...
all	alle; alles
All Hallows' Eve	*(der) Abend vor Allerheiligen*
almost	fast; beinahe
alone	allein
along	entlang
already	schon; bereits
also	auch
although	obwohl
always	immer
am (= ante meridiem)	morgens, vormittags *(hinter Uhrzeit)*
and	und
angry	zornig, wütend
animal	(das) Tier
announcement	(die) Mitteilung; (die) Durchsage
annoyed	genervt
another	noch ein/noch eine; ein anderer/ ein anderes/eine andere
any	(irgend)ein(e)
anything else	noch etwas
any more, anymore	noch mehr
not anymore	nicht mehr
apple	(der) Apfel
apple bobbing	*(das) Apfelfischen*
area	(das) Gebiet; (die) Region
around	um; herum; umher

What is it about?
Worum geht es?

(irr) bedeutet: Dies ist ein unregelmäßiges Verb. Du findest die Formen auf den Seiten 146 und 147. !

all over the world auf der ganzen Welt
all the time die ganze Zeit
all the work die ganze Arbeit
all year round das ganze Jahr lang

There are **animals** at a zoo.

apple

(to) **arrest**	verhaften
(to) **arrive**	ankommen
art	(die) Kunst
arts and crafts	(das) Basteln; (die) Bastelarbeit
as	als; wie; während
as … as	so … wie
(to) **ask**	fragen; bitten
(to) **ask for**	bitten um
(to) **ask questions**	Fragen stellen
at	an; in; bei; um
athlete	(der) Athlet / (die) Athletin
(to) **attack**	angreifen
attraction	(die) Attraktion
August	(der) August
aunt	(die) Tante
Australia	Australien
autumn	(der) Herbst
away	weg

at all times jederzeit
at first zuerst
at home zu Hause
at the back hinten
at the end am Ende
at the weekend am Wochenende
at this time zu dieser Zeit

B

B&B (= bed and breakfast)	(die) Frühstückspension
back	zurück
at the back	hinten
background	(der) Hintergrund
bad	schlecht; schlimm
(to) **bake**	backen
baker	(der) Bäcker / (die) Bäckerin
baking paper	(das) Backpapier
balloon	(der) Luftballon
banana	(die) Banane
barbecue	(der) Grill; (die) Grillparty
bark	(die) Rinde; (die) Borke
basking shark	(der) Riesenhai
bathroom	(das) Badezimmer
battery	(die) Batterie
(to) **be** *(irr)*	sein
(to) **be afraid of** *(irr)*	Angst haben vor
(to) **be allowed (to)** *(irr)*	erlaubt sein, dürfen
(to) **be forgot** *(irr, poetisch)*	vergessen werden
(to) **be fun** *(irr)*	Spaß machen
(to) **be good at something** *(irr)*	gut in etwas sein
(to) **be right** *(irr)*	recht haben
beach	(der) Strand
beautiful, beautifully	schön
because	weil; da
(to) **become** *(irr)*	werden

banana

there is / there are es gibt, dort ist / es gibt, dort sind
there was / were es gab, dort war / es gab, dort waren
there will be es wird geben
there won't be es wird nicht geben
Are there …? Gibt es …?

bed	(das) Bett
bedroom	(das) Schlafzimmer
bee	(die) Biene
before	bevor; vor
beginning	(der) Anfang; (der) Beginn
(to) **believe (in)**	glauben (an)
bell	(die) Glocke
below	unten, unter
best, the best	beste(r, s), der/die/das beste
better	besser
between	zwischen
big	groß
bike	(das) Fahrrad
(to) **ride a bike**	Fahrrad fahren
birthday	(der) Geburtstag
biscuit	(der) Keks
blood	(das) Blut
blue	blau
board game	(das) Brettspiel
boat	(das) Boot
boiling	kochend
bonfire	(das) (Freuden)feuer
Bonfire Night	*britisches Gedenkfest am 5. November*
book	(das) Buch
(to) **book**	buchen, reservieren
bookshelf (*pl* **bookshelves**)	(das) Bücherregal
bored	gelangweilt
boring	langweilig
bottle	(die) Flasche
bowl	(die) Schüssel; (die) Schale
boy	(der) Junge
bread	(das) Brot
(to) **break** *(irr)*	brechen
breakfast	(das) Frühstück
bridge	(die) Brücke
bright, brightly	strahlend, hell
brilliant	genial, klasse
(to) **bring** *(irr)*	bringen, mitbringen
Britain	Großbritannien
British	britisch
brochure	(die) Broschüre
broken	gebrochen
brother	(der) Bruder
brown	braun
(to) **build** *(irr)*	bauen
building	(das) Gebäude
busy	belebt; verkehrsreich

bee

bigger größer
the biggest der/die/das größte

boat

a **bottle** of orange juice

bridge

This is a modern **building**.

but	aber	
butterfly	(der) Schmetterling	**butterfly** 
(to) **buy** *(irr)*	kaufen	
by	von; mit; bei, an; (spätestens) bis	
by heart	auswendig	

C

cage	(der) Käfig	
cake	(der) Kuchen	
(to) **call**	anrufen	
(to) **be called**	heißen, genannt werden	
camera	(die) Kamera; (der) Fotoapparat	 **camera**
camp	(das) (Zelt)lager	
campsite	(der) Campingplatz	
can	können	
can't (= **cannot**)	nicht können	
candle	(die) Kerze	**candles** 
candle holder	(der) Kerzenständer	
cap	(die) Mütze	
capsule	(die) Kapsel	
car	(das) Auto	
car park	(der) Parkplatz	
caravan	(der) Wohnwagen	
careful, carefully	vorsichtig	
carnival	(der) Karneval	
(to) **carve**	schnitzen	
case	(der) Fall	
castle	(die) Burg; (das) Schloss	
cat	(die) Katze	 **cat**
cat food	(das) Katzenfutter	
(to) **catch up with**	*sich nach längerer Zeit (auch virtuell) mit jemandem treffen, um sich auf den neuesten Stand zu bringen*	
category	(die) Kategorie	
Catholic	(der) Katholik / (die) Katholikin; katholisch	
(to) **celebrate**	feiern	
celebration	(die) Feier	
cellar	(der) Keller	
centre	(das) Zentrum	
century	(das) Jahrhundert	a **century** = 100 years
chain	(die) Kette	
(to) **change**	(sich) ändern; verändern; wechseln	
character	(die) Figur; (der) Charakter	
(to) **check**	überprüfen; kontrollieren	
(to) **check out**	sich ansehen; ausprobieren	

checklist	(die) Checkliste
chef	(der) Koch / (die) Köchin
chicken	(das) Huhn
child (*pl* **children**)	(das) Kind
chocolate	(die) Schokolade
(to) **choose** *(irr)*	wählen; sich entscheiden
chore	(die) lästige Aufgabe; (die) Hausarbeit
Christian	(der Christ / (die) Christin; christlich
Christmas	(das) Weihnachten
cinema	(das) Kino
city	(die) Stadt; (die) Innenstadt
(to) **clang**	scheppern, klappern
class	(die) Klasse; (die) Unterrichtsstunde
classroom	(das) Klassenzimmer
(to) **clean (up)**	sauber machen
clear, clearly	klar; deutlich
clever	klug; schlau
(to) **climb**	auf etwas (hinauf)steigen; klettern
clock	(die) Uhr
clock tower	(der) Uhrenturm
(to) **clonk**	scheppern, klappern
(to) **close**	zumachen; schließen
closed	geschlossen
clothes *(pl)*	(die) Kleider; (die) Kleidung
cm (= centimetre)	(der) Zentimeter
coach	(der) Trainer / (die) Trainerin
coast	(die) Küste
coin	(die) Münze
cold	kalt; (die) Kälte
(to) **collect**	sammeln
collection	(die) Sammlung
colour	(die) Farbe; färben
come *(irr)*	kommen
(to) **come back** *(irr)*	zurückkommen
compass	(der) Kompass
(to) **cook**	braten; backen; kochen
cooking	(das) Kochen; Koch-
(to) **do the cooking** *(irr)*	kochen
(to) **cool**	abkühlen
corner	(die) Ecke
correct	richtig, korrekt
(to) **cost**	kosten
costume	(das) Kostüm
could	könnte(st, n, t); konnte(st, n, t)
country	(das) Land
a couple of	einige, ein paar

chicken

(pl) bedeutet:
Dies ist ein Wort in der Mehrzahl.

clock

coast

to **do the cooking**

course	(der) Kurs
cousin	(der) Cousin / (die) Cousine
(to) **cover**	bedecken
cow	(die) Kuh
crash	*hier:* (der) Krach; (das) Getöse
crazy	verrückt; wahnsinnig
(to) **create**	erschaffen; erzeugen
creative	kreativ
criminal	(der) Verbrecher / (die) Verbrecherin
crisps *(pl)*	(die) Chips
(to) **cross**	überqueren
(to) **cry**	weinen; schreien
cuddly	knuddelig
customer	(der) Kunde / (die) Kundin
(to) **cut** *(irr)*	schneiden
(to) **cycle**	Rad fahren, radeln
(to) **go cycling**	Rad fahren gehen

cow

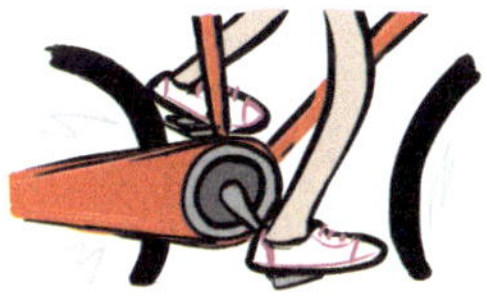

to **go cycling**, to **cycle**

D

dad	(der) Papa; (der) Vati
(to) **dance**	tanzen
dancing	(das) Tanzen
dangerous, dangerously	gefährlich
dark	dunkel; (die) Dunkelheit
date	(das) Datum
daughter	(die) Tochter
day	(der) Tag
one day	eines Tages
day out	(der) Ausflugstag
deadline	(der) letzte Termin; (die) Deadline
dear	liebe/r *(Anrede)*
December	(der) Dezember
(to) **decorate**	schmücken; dekorieren
decoration	(der) Schmuck, (die) Dekoration
deer	(der) Hirsch; (das) Reh
delicious	köstlich, lecker
(to) **describe**	beschreiben
design	(der) Entwurf; entwerfen
desk	(der) Schreibtisch
detective	(der) Detektiv / (die) Detektivin
dialogue	(das) Gespräch; (der) Dialog
diary	(das) Tagebuch
different	anders; andere(r, s); verschiedene(r, s)
difficult	schwierig; schwer
dinner	(das) Abendessen
dinosaur	(der) Dinosaurier

dancing

desk

(to) **disappear**	verschwinden
(to) **discover**	entdecken
(to) **discuss**	besprechen; diskutieren
discussion	(die) Diskussion
dishwasher	(die) Spülmaschine
(to) **do** *(irr)*	tun; machen
(to) **do sports** *(irr)*	Sport treiben
(to) **do the cooking** *(irr)*	kochen
(to) **like to do something**	etwas gern tun
doctor	(der) Arzt / (die) Ärztin
dog	(der) Hund
dog food	(das) Hundefutter
door	(die) Tür
double-decker (bus)	(der) Doppeldecker(bus)
down	hinunter; (nach) unten
Dr (= Doctor)	Dr. (= der Doktor / die Doktorin)
drama	Theater-; Schauspiel-
(to) **draw** *(irr)*	zeichnen
drawing	(die) Zeichnung
dream	(der) Traum
(to) **dress up**	(sich) verkleiden
drink	(das) Trinken; (das) Getränk
(to) **drink**	trinken
(to) **drive** *(irr)*	fahren
dry	trocken; trocknen
during	während

dishwasher

dog

to **drink**

E

each	jede(r, s)
each other	einander
early	früh
earth	(die) Erde
Easter	(das) Ostern
Easter bunny	(der) Osterhase
Easter egg	(das) Osterei
Easter egg hunt	(die) Ostereiersuche
Easter egg roll	*(das) Ostereierrollen*
easy	leicht; einfach
eat *(irr)*	essen
egg	(das) Ei
Egyptian	ägyptisch
anything else	noch etwas
something else	etwas anderes
(to) **empty**	ausleeren; ausräumen
end, ending	(das) Ende; (der) Schluss
engineer	(der) Ingenieur / (die) Ingenieurin
English	(das) Englisch; englisch

earlier vorhin, früher

Easter eggs

eggs

at the end / in the end
am Ende, schließlich

(to) **enjoy**	genießen	
enough	genug	
entertainment	(die) Unterhaltung	
entrance	(der) Eingang; (der) Eintritt	
entry	(der) Eintritt, (der) Eingang	
environment	(die) Umwelt; (die) Umgebung	
especially	besonders; vor allem	
Europe	(das) Europa	
New Year's Eve	(das) Silvester	
even	selbst; sogar	
evening	(der) Abend	**in the evening** am Abend
ever	jemals	
every	jede(r, s)	
everybody	alle; jeder	
everybody else	jede/r andere	
everyday	alltäglich, Alltags-	
everyone	alle; jeder	
except	außer	
excited	aufgeregt	
exciting	aufregend	
excuse me	Entschuldigung!	
exercise	(die) Übung	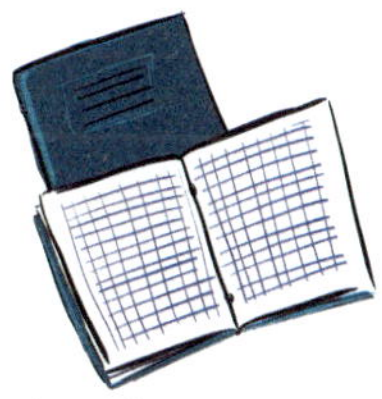
exercise book	(das) Heft	**exercise book**
exhibition	(die) Ausstellung	
(to) **exist**	existieren	
expensive	teuer	
experience	(die) Erfahrung	
experiment	(das) Experiment; (der) Versuch	
(to) **express**	ausdrücken	

F

face	(das) Gesicht	
face painting	(die) Gesichtsbemalung	
(to) **fall down** *(irr)*	hinfallen	**more famous** berühmter
false	falsch	**(the) most famous**
family	(die) Familie	der/die/das berühmteste;
famous	berühmt	am berühmtesten
fancy	nobel	
fantastic	fantastisch; super	
farm	(der) Bauernhof	
fashion	(die) Mode	**faster** schneller
fast	schnell	
fat	(das) Fett	
father	(der) Vater	
favourite	(der) Liebling; Lieblings-	
February	(der) Februar	
(to) **feed** *(irr)*	füttern	

feeder	(die) Futterstation
feeding time	(die) Fütterungszeit
(to) **feel** *(irr)*	(sich) fühlen
felt-tip	(der) Filzstift
ferris wheel	(das) Riesenrad
festival	(das) Fest; (das) Festival
fever	(das) Fieber
a few	einige; wenige
field	(das) Feld
field trip	(die) Exkursion
(to) **fight** *(irr)*	bekämpfen; ankämpfen gegen
(to) **fill**	füllen
(to) **film**	drehen, filmen
(to) **filter**	filtern
(to) **find** *(irr)*	finden
(to) **find out** *(irr)*	herausfinden
fingerprint	(der) Fingerabdruck
(to) **finish**	beenden; enden; fertigstellen
fire	(das) Feuer
firefighter	(der) Feuerwehrmann / (die) Feuerwehrfrau
firework show	(das) Feuerwerk
fireworks (display)	(das) Feuerwerk
first	zuerst; erste(r, s)
for the first time	zum ersten Mal
first footing	*(das) Abstatten eines Neujahrs-besuchs (schottische Tradition)*
first of all	zuallererst
fish	(der) Fisch
flag	(die) Fahne; (die) Flagge
floor	(der) Fußboden
flower	(die) Blume
(to) **fly** *(irr)*	fliegen
food	(das) Essen; (das) Futter
foot (*pl* **feet**)	(der) Fuß
football	(der) Fußball, (das) Fußballspiel
for	für
for *(+ Zeitraum)*	... lang
for example	zum Beispiel
for the first time	zum ersten Mal
forest	(der) Wald
(to) **forget**	vergessen
fort	(das) Fort; (die) Festung
fox	(der) Fuchs
France	Frankreich
free	frei; kostenlos
free time	(die) Freizeit

felt-tip

The **firefighters** are fighting the **fire**.

flower

football

fox

fresh	frisch; neu
Friday	(der) Freitag
(on) **Fridays**	freitags
friend	(der) Freund / (die) Freundin
friendly	freundlich
(to) **frighten**	erschrecken
frogs' legs *(pl)*	(die) Froschschenkel *(pl)*
from	von; aus
in front of	vor
fruit	(die) Frucht; (das) Obst
frustrated	frustriert
full of	voller
fun	(der) Spaß; lustig; witzig
(to) **be fun** *(irr)*	Spaß machen
(to) **have (a lot of) fun** *(irr)*	(viel) Spaß haben
funfair	(die) Kirmes; (der) Vergnügungspark
funny	lustig
further	weiter
future	(die) Zukunft; zukünftig

friends

fruit

G

g (= gram)	(das) Gramm
game	(das) Spiel
garden	(der) Garten
gardener	(der) Gärtner / (die) Gärtnerin
gate	(das) Tor
German	(das) Deutsch; deutsch
(to) **get** *(irr)*	bekommen; kommen; gelangen; werden; holen; kaufen
(to) **get along** *(irr)*	sich verstehen
(to) **get up** *(irr)*	aufstehen
ghost	(der) Geist; (das) Gespenst
ghostly	geisterhaft; gespenstisch
girl	(das) Mädchen
(to) **give** *(irr)*	geben
(to) **give directions** *(irr)*	den Weg beschreiben
glass	(das) Glas
glasses *(pl)*	(die) Brille
(to) **glow**	leuchten, glühen
(to) **go** *(irr)*	gehen; fahren
(to) **go abroad** *(irr)*	ins Ausland fahren
(to) **go away** *(irr)*	weggehen; verschwinden
(to) **go camping** *(irr)*	zelten gehen
(to) **go cycling** *(irr)*	Rad fahren gehen
(to) **go hiking** *(irr)*	wandern gehen
(to) **go on** *(irr)*	passieren
(to) **go out** *(irr)*	(hinaus)gehen; ausgehen

ghost

The children wear **glasses**.

(to) **go riding** *(irr)*	reiten gehen
(to) **go shopping** *(irr)*	einkaufen gehen
(to) **go swimming** *(irr)*	schwimmen gehen
(to) **go with** *(irr)*	gehören zu; passen zu
thank God	Gott sei Dank
(to) **be going to do something** *(irr)*	etwas tun werden
gone	weg
good	gut
(to) **be good at something** *(irr)*	gut in etwas sein
good luck	(das) Glück
goodbye	auf Wiedersehen
grammar	(die) Grammatik
grandfather	(der) Großvater
grandma *(informal)*	(die) Oma
grandmother	(die) Großmutter
grandpa *(informal)*	(der) Opa
grandparents *(pl)*	(die) Großeltern
granny *(informal)*	(die) Oma
grape	(die) (Wein)traube
grass	(das) Gras
great	groß; großartig
green	grün
(to) **grill**	grillen
ground	(der) Boden
group	(die) Gruppe
(to) **grow up** *(irr)*	erwachsen sein, erwachsen werden
(to) **guess**	(er)raten
guest	(der) Gast
guide	(der) Führer / (die) Führerin
guided	geführt
guitar	(die) Gitarre
gunpowder	(das) Schießpulver
(you) guys *(pl, informal)*	(die) Leute *(umgangssprachlich)*

You can **go swimming** at a swimming pool.

grapes

(informal) bedeutet: Dies ist ein umgangssprachliches Wort.

guitar

H

hair	(das) Haar; (die) Haare
hairdresser	(der) Friseur / (die) Friseurin
half	halb
half (*pl* **halves**)	(die) Hälfte
(to) **hand in**	einreichen; abgeben
(to) **hang** *(irr)*	hängen
(to) **hang up** *(irr)*	(auf)hängen
happy	glücklich
happily	glücklich(erweise)
hard	hart, schwierig

hair

Happy New Year!
Frohes Neues Jahr!

hat	(der) Hut
(to) **hate**	hassen; nicht ausstehen können
(to) **have** *(irr)*	haben; essen; trinken
(to) **have a look** *(irr)*	nachsehen
(to) **have a look at** *(irr)*	sich ansehen
(to) **have (a lot of) fun** *(irr)*	(viel) Spaß haben
(to) **have a picnic** *(irr)*	ein Picknick machen
(to) **have got** *(irr)*	haben
(to) **have put together** *(irr)*	zusammengestellt haben
(to) **have to** *(irr)*	müssen
he	er
headteacher	(der) Schulleiter / (die) Schulleiterin; (der) Rektor / (die) Rektorin
healthy	gesund
heart	(das) Herz
by heart	auswendig
hedgehog	(der) Igel
height	(die) Höhe
helicopter	(der) Hubschrauber
hello	hallo
help	(die) Hilfe; helfen
her	ihr/ihre; sie
here	hier; hierher
(to) **hide** *(irr)*	(sich) verstecken
high	hoch
(to) **hike**	wandern
him	ihm, ihn
(to) **hire**	mieten
his	sein; seine(r, s)
history	(die) Geschichte
hole	(das) Loch
holiday	(der) Feiertag
holiday(s)	(die) Ferien; (der) Urlaub
hologram	(das) Hologramm
home	(das) Zuhause; (das) Haus; zu Hause; daheim; nach Hause
homework	(die) Hausaufgaben
(to) **hope**	hoffen
horse	(das) Pferd
horse riding	(das) Reiten
hospital	(das) Krankenhaus
hot	heiß
hot chocolate	(der) heiße Kakao
house	(das) Haus
houseboat	(das) Hausboot
how	wie
huge	riesig
hungry	hungrig

to **have a picnic**

heart

here's (= here is) hier ist

at home zu Hause

horse

How are you?
Wie geht es dir? /
Wie geht es euch? /
Wie geht es Ihnen?

I

I	ich
idea	(die) Idee; (die) Vorstellung
if	ob; wenn; falls
ill	krank
important	wichtig
impossible	unmöglich
(to) **improve**	verbessern; besser werden
in	in; auf
in front of	vor
in the end	am Ende, schließlich
in the evening	am Abend
in the morning	am Morgen
(to) **include**	beinhalten; einbeziehen
(to) **inform**	informieren
information *(no pl)*	(die) Informationen
insect	(das) Insekt
inside	innerhalb; innen; drinnen; hinein
inspector	(der) Inspektor / (die) Inspektorin
interested	interessiert
(to) **be interested in** *(irr)*	interessiert sein an
interesting	interessant
(to) **interrupt**	unterbrechen
into	in
(to) **invent**	erfinden
invitation	(die) Einladung
(to) **invite**	einladen
Ireland	Irland
Irish	irisch
is made	wird gemacht
it	es
Italian	(der) Italiener / (die) Italienerin; italienisch
Italy	Italien
its	sein(e), ihr(e) *(sächlich)*

I'd like to ... Ich würde gern ...
I'll (= I will) ich werde
I'm (= I am) ich bin, ich heiße
I've looked (= I have looked) ich habe geguckt

insects

invitation

it's (= it is) es ist; es gibt

J

jack-o'-lantern	(die) Kürbislaterne
jacket	(die) Jacke
jacket potato	(die) Ofenkartoffel; (die) Folienkartoffel
Jewish	jüdisch
job	(die) Aufgabe; (der) Beruf
(to) **join**	mitmachen (bei)
(to) **join in**	sich beteiligen an; mitmachen bei
juice	(der) Saft

jack-o'-lantern

just	nur; einfach; wirklich; genau; gerade

K

(to) **keep** *(irr)*	halten; behalten; aufbewahren
key	(der) Schlüssel
kg (= **kilogram**)	(das) Kilogramm
(to) **kick**	treten
kid	(das) Kind
kind	(die) Art; (die) Sorte
king	(der) König
knife (*pl* **knives**)	(das) Messer
(to) **know** *(irr)*	wissen; kennen

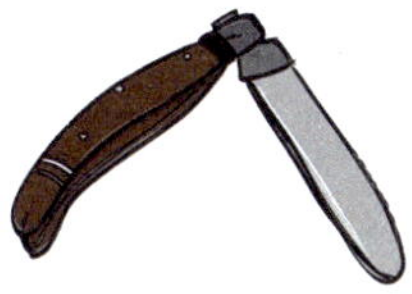

knife

L

lab	(das) Labor
lamp	(die) Lampe
language	(die) Sprache
large	groß
the largest	der/die/das größte; am größten
last	letzte(r, s)
late	(zu) spät
later	später
laughter	(das) Gelächter; (das) Lachen
lazy	faul
leaf (*pl* **leaves**)	(das) Blatt
(to) **learn** *(irr)*	lernen
(to) **leave** *(irr)*	(übrig) lassen; zurücklassen; verlassen, abfahren; weggehen
on the left / on your left	links, auf der / deiner linken Seite
leg	(das) Bein
lemon	(die) Zitrone
lemonade	(die) Limonade
lesson	(die) Stunde; (der) Unterricht
(to) **let** *(irr)*	lassen
letter	(der) Buchstabe; (der) Brief
library	(die) Bücherei
life (*pl* **lives**)	(das) Leben
lift	(der) Aufzug
light *(irr)*	(das) Licht; anzünden
lighting	(die) Beleuchtung
like	wie
(to) **like**	mögen
(to) **like to do something** / (to) **like doing something**	etwas gern tun
line	(die) Linie; (die) Zeile
linking word	(das) Verbindungswort

lamp

they've left
sie haben zurückgelassen

let's (= **let us**) lass(t) uns

I'd like to ...
Ich würde gern ...
What is it like? Wie ist es?
What was that like?
Wie war das?

lion	(der) Löwe
list	(die) Liste
(to) **listen (to)**	zuhören, anhören
little	klein
(to) **live**	leben; wohnen
living room	(das) Wohnzimmer
lonely	einsam
long	lang
(to) **look**	aussehen; (an)sehen, (an)schauen
(to) **look after**	sich kümmern um; aufpassen auf
(to) **look (at)**	(an)sehen, (an)schauen
(to) **look for**	suchen nach
(to) **look forward to**	sich freuen auf
(to) **have a look** *(irr)*	nachsehen
(to) **have a look at** *(irr)*	sich ansehen
a lot	viel, sehr
a lot (of) / lots	viel(e), jede Menge
lots of	viel(e)
loud, loudly	laut
love	viele Grüße; alles Liebe *(in Briefen)*
(to) **love**	lieben, sehr mögen
good luck	(das) Glück
lunch	(das) Mittagessen

lion

longer länger
the longest der/die/das längste

M

magic, magical	magisch
(to) **make** *(irr)*	machen
(to) **make sure** *(irr)*	darauf achten, dass ...
man (*pl* **men**)	(der) Mann
many	viele
map	(die) Karte
March	(der) März
market	(der) Markt
married	verheiratet
masterpiece	(das) Meisterwerk
match	(das) Spiel
May	(der) Mai
may	können; dürfen
maybe	vielleicht
me, to me	mir; mich; ich
mechanic	(der) Mechaniker / (die) Mechanikerin
(to) **meet** *(irr)*	kennenlernen; (sich) treffen
meeting	(die) Versammlung; Treffen
(to) **melt**	schmelzen
member	(das) Mitglied
memorial	(das) Denkmal; (das) Ehrenmal
message	(die) Nachricht; (die) Botschaft

is made wird gemacht

map

memorial

metal	(das) Metall
metre (= m)	(der) Meter
Mexican	mexikanisch
microscope	(das) Mikroskop
midnight	(die) Mitternacht
mile	(die) Meile
milk	(die) Milch; melken
milkshake	(der) Milchshake
(to) **change one's mind**	seine Meinung ändern
(to) **miss**	vermissen; verpassen
(to) **mix**	sich (ver)mischen
ml (= **millilitre**)	(der) Milliliter
mobile (phone)	(das) Handy
model	(das) Modell
Monday	(der) Montag
money	(das) Geld
month	(der) Monat
mood	(die) Laune; (die) Stimmung
moon	(der) Mond
more	mehr; weitere
morning	(der) Morgen
in the morning	am Morgen
mosque	(die) Moschee
moss	(das) Moos
mountain	(der) Berg
mountaintop	(der) Berggipfel
mouth	(der) Mund
(to) **move**	umziehen
Mr	Herr *(Anrede)*
Mrs	Frau *(Anrede)*
much	viel; sehr
mum, Mum	(die) Mama; (die) Mutti
mummy (*pl* **mummies**)	(die) Mumie
music	(die) Musik
musician	(der) Musiker / (die) Musikerin
Muslim	(der) Muslim / (die) Muslimin; muslimisch
must	(das) Muss; müssen
mustn't (= **must not**)	nicht dürfen
my	mein(e)

microscope

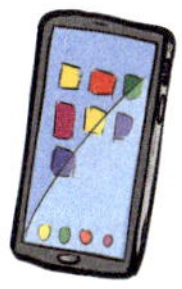

mobile phone

more beautiful schöner
more expensive teurer
more famous berühmter
more fantastic fantastischer
more important wichtiger
more interesting interessanter
the most beautiful der/die/das schönste
the most expensive der/die/das teuerste; am teuersten
the most famous der/die/das berühmteste; am berühmtesten
the most fantastic der/die/das fantastischste; am fantastischsten
the most interesting der/die/das interessanteste; am interessantesten
the most popular der/die/das beliebteste; am beliebtesten

N

nail	(der) Nagel
the Natural History Museum	(das) Naturkundemuseum
near	nahe, in der Nähe von
the nearest	der/die/das nächste; am nächsten

nearly	fast; beinahe
(to) **need**	brauchen
neighbour	(der) Nachbar / (die) Nachbarin
neighbourhood	(das) Viertel; (die) Nachbarschaft
never	nie, niemals
new	neu
new year	(das) Neujahr
New Year's Day	(der) Neujahrstag
New Year's Eve	(das) Silvester
newspaper	(die) Zeitung
next	nächste(r, s); dann, als Nächstes
next to	neben
nice	schön; nett
night	(die) Nacht; (der) Abend
no	kein(e); nein
no one	keiner
noise	(das) Geräusch; (der) Lärm
not	nicht
not anymore	nicht mehr
not yet	noch nicht
note	(die) Nachricht; (die) Notiz
(to) **note**	beachten, zur Kenntnis nehmen
noticeboard	(das) Schwarze Brett
November	(der) November
now	jetzt
number	(die) Zahl; (die) Nummer; (die) Anzahl
nurse	(die) Krankenschwester; (der) Krankenpfleger
nut	(die) Nuss

newspaper

No, I haven't. Nein.
No, I'm not. Nein.
No, you can't. Nein.

noticeboard

nurse

O

o'clock	Uhr *(bei Nennung einer Uhrzeit)*
object	(der) Gegenstand
October	(der) Oktober
odd one out	*(das) Wort, das nicht zu den anderen passt*
of	von; aus
of course	natürlich
office	(das) Büro
often	oft; häufig
oh dear	oje
old	alt
on	auf; an; in; *auch:* über
on the left	links, auf der linken Seite
on time	pünktlich
on your left	links, auf deiner linken Seite

older älter
the oldest der/die/das älteste; am ältesten

on your right	rechts, auf deiner rechten Seite
one	ein(e); eins
one day	eines Tages
only	nur, bloß; erst
onto	auf, in
open	offen; geöffnet; öffnen; aufmachen
open-air	im Freien
opening	(die) Öffnung; (die) Eröffnung
opinion	(die) Meinung; (die) Ansicht
or	oder
orange	orange; (die) Orange; (die) Apfelsine
(to) **organize (= organise)**	organisieren
other	andere(r, s)
our	unser(e, r, s)
out	draußen; heraus, hinaus; aus
out and about	unterwegs
out of	aus
outdoor	im Freien
outside	draußen; außen; (nach) draußen
over	über, hinüber; vorbei
over there	dort (drüben)
overstuffed	*zu prall ausgestopft*
own	eigene(r, s)
owner	(der) Besitzer / (die) Besitzerin

orange

outdoor

P

packed lunch	(das) Lunchpaket
(to) **paint**	(an)malen
painted	bemalt, farbig
pair	(das) Paar
paper	(das) Papier
parents *(pl)*	(die) Eltern
parking	(das) Parken
part	(der) Teil
past	vorbei; vorüber; nach; (die) Vergangenheit
(to) **pay** *(irr)*	(be)zahlen
pen	(der) Stift
pencil	(der) Bleistift
people	(die) Leute; (die) Menschen
perfect	perfekt
(to) **perform**	aufführen; durchführen
performance	(die) Aufführung; (die) Leistung
pet	(das) Haustier
phew *(informal)*	puh
phone	(das) Telefon

a piece of **paper**

pencil

photo	(das) Foto
(to) **take a photo** *(irr)*	ein Foto machen
photographer	(der) Fotograf / (die) Fotografin
picnic	(das) Picknick
(to) **have a picnic** *(irr)*	ein Picknick machen
picture	(das) Bild
(to) **take a picture** *(irr)*	ein Foto machen
piece	(das) Stück; (das) Teil
pinecone	(der) Kiefernzapfen
pipe	(die) Pfeife
place	(der) Ort; (der) Platz; (das) Haus, (das) Zuhause; platzieren; stellen
(to) **plan**	planen
plane	(das) Flugzeug
(to) **plant**	pflanzen
plastic	(das) Plastik
plastic bottle	(die) Plastikflasche
platform	(der) Bahnsteig; (die) Plattform
(to) **play**	spielen
play	(das) Spiel; (das) (Theater)stück
playing	(das) Spielen
please	bitte
plot	(die) Verschwörung
pm (= post meridiem)	nachmittags; abends *(hinter Uhrzeit)*
pocket money	(das) Taschengeld
poem	(das) Gedicht
point	(der) Punkt
Poland	Polen
police officer	(der) Polizeibeamte / (die) Polizeibeamtin
polite, politely	höflich
popular	beliebt
postcard	(die) Postkarte; (die) Ansichtskarte
pot	(der) Topf
pound (= £)	(das) Pfund *(brit. Währung)*
practice	(die) Übung; (das) Training
(to) **practise**	üben; trainieren
prediction	(die) Vorhersage; (die) Prophezeiung
present	(das) Geschenk; (die) Gegenwart
present perfect	*(das) Perfekt*
present progressive	*(die) Verlaufsform der Gegenwart*
(to) **present (to)**	präsentieren, vorstellen
probably	wahrscheinlich
professional	professionell; beruflich
programme	(das) Programm
project	(das) Projekt

to **take a photo**

plane

police officer

postcard

presents

prop	(die) Requisite
(to) **protect**	beschützen
proud, proudly	stolz
public	öffentlich
pumpkin	(der) Kürbis
(to) **push**	schieben; stoßen
(to) **put** *(irr)*	setzen; stellen; legen; stecken
(to) **put together** *(irr)*	zusammenstellen; zusammensetzen

pumpkin

Q

queen	(die) Königin
question	(die) Frage
(to) **ask questions**	Fragen stellen
quickly	schnell
quiet	leise; ruhig
quite	ziemlich

quickly = fast

R

rabbit	(das) Kaninchen
rain	(der) Regen
rainy	regnerisch
(to) **rattle**	klappern; rasseln
(to) **read** *(irr)*	lesen
real	wirklich; echt
really	wirklich
reason	(der) Grund
recipe	(das) Rezept
(to) **record**	aufnehmen
red	rot
regular	üblich, normal
relative	(der) Verwandte / (die) Verwandte
relaxed	entspannt
religion	(die) Religion
religious	religiöse(r, s)
(to) **remember**	sich erinnern an
(to) **renovate**	renovieren
(to) **report**	sich melden
respect	(der) Respekt
(to) **respect**	respektieren
rice	(der) Reis
(to) **ride** *(irr)*	fahren; reiten
(to) **ride a bike** *(irr)*	Fahrrad fahren
(to) **go riding** *(irr)*	reiten gehen
(to) **be right** *(irr)*	recht haben
right	rechts, nach rechts; genau; direkt
on your right	rechts, auf deiner rechten Seite

we've read (= we have read)
wir haben gelesen

to **ride a bike**

right now	jetzt; sofort; gleich; im Moment
(to) **ring** *(irr)*	klingeln; läuten; *hier:* Glockenläuten
river	(der) Fluss
road	(die) Straße
(to) **roast**	rösten, braten
robot	(der) Roboter
rocket	(die) Rakete
role	(die) Rolle
roll	(die) Rolle
Roman	(der) Römer / (die) Römerin; römisch
Rome	Rom
room	(der) Raum; (das) Zimmer
all year round	das ganze Jahr lang
roundhouse	(das) Rundhaus
rubbish	(der) Müll
rule	(die) Regel
run	(der) Lauf
(to) **run** *(irr)*	laufen; rennen; leiten, betreiben; *auch:* fließen
(to) run away *(irr)*	weglaufen

robot

He is taking out the **rubbish**.

S

sad, sadly	traurig
safe	sicher; ungefährlich
safety	(die) Sicherheit
salad	(der) Salat
salt	(das) Salz
the same	der/die/das Gleiche; derselbe/dieselbe/dasselbe
Saturday	(der) Samstag
(on) Saturdays	samstags
sausage	(die) Wurst; (das) Würstchen
(to) **save**	*hier:* zurücklegen lassen
(to) **say** *(irr)*	sagen
(to) **scare**	erschrecken
(to) **scare away**	verscheuchen
scared	verängstigt, ängstlich
(to) **be scared (of)** *(irr)*	Angst haben (vor)
scary	Furcht erregend
scene	(die) Szene
school	(die) Schule
school grounds *(pl)*	(das) Schulgelände
science	(die) Naturwissenschaft
the Science Museum	(das) Naturwissenschaftsmuseum
Scotland	Schottland
Scottish	schottisch
screen	(der) Bildschirm

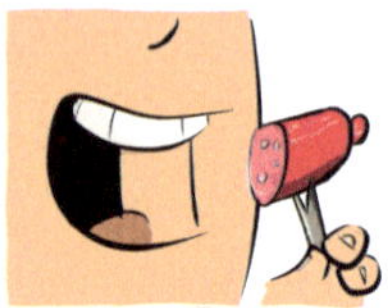

He is eating a **sausage**.

screen

script	(das) Drehbuch; (das) Skript	
sea	(das) Meer; (die) See	
seaside	(die) (Meeres)küste; (das) Meer	
second	zweite(r, s); (die) Sekunde	
the second largest	der/die/das zweitgrößte	
second-hand	gebraucht	
(to) **see** *(irr)*	sehen; *auch:* verstehen	**I see.** Ich verstehe. **See u.** (= **See you!**) Bis bald! **Have you ever seen ...?** Hast du jemals ... gesehen?
seed	(der) Samen	
(to) **send** *(irr)*	schicken	
(to) **set the table** *(irr)*	den Tisch decken	
she	sie	
sheet	(das) Blatt; (der) Bogen	
shelf (*pl* **shelves**)	(das) Regal	
shirt	(das) Hemd	
shoe	(der) Schuh	
shop	(das) Geschäft; (der) Laden	
shop assistant	(der) Verkäufer / (die) Verkäuferin	
shopping	(das) Einkaufen; Einkaufs-	
shopping centre	(das) Einkaufszentrum	
short	kurz	**shorter** kürzer **the shortest** der/die/das kürzeste
should	sollte(st, n, t)	
(to) **show** *(irr)*	zeigen	
sick	krank	
side	(die) Seite	
sight	(die) Sehenswürdigkeit	
sign	(das) Zeichen; (das) Schild	
(to) **sign up**	sich anmelden	
simple past	*(die) einfache Vergangenheit*	
since	seit	
yours sincerely	mit freundlichen Grüßen *(am Ende eines formellen Briefes)*	
(to) **sing** *(irr)*	singen	
singer	(der) Sänger / (die) Sängerin	 **singer**
singing	singend	
Sir	Sir; Herr *(Anrede vor Vornamen)*	
sister	(die) Schwester	
(to) **sit** *(irr)*	sitzen	
size	(die) Größe	
skeleton	(das) Skelett	
skewer	(der) Spieß	
skirt	(der) Rock	 **skirt**
skyscraper	(der) Wolkenkratzer	
(to) **sleep** *(irr)*	schlafen	
(to) **sleep in** *(irr)*	ausschlafen	
slow, slowly	langsam	
small	klein	**smaller** kleiner **the smallest** der/die/das kleinste
smart	schlau, clever	

smelly	stinkend
(to) **smile**	lächeln
snail	(die) Schnecke
snake	(die) Schlange
so	deshalb; daher; also
so that	damit
sock	(die) Socke
soft	weich
solar-powered	solarbetrieben
solution	(die) Lösung
(to) **solve**	lösen
some	einige, ein paar; etwas
someone	jemand; irgendwer
something	etwas
something else	etwas anderes
sometimes	manchmal
somewhere	irgendwo
son	(der) Sohn
song	(das) Lied
sound	(das) Geräusch; (der) Klang
(to) **sound**	klingen, sich anhören
space capsule	(die) Weltraumkapsel
Spain	Spanien
sparkler	(die) Wunderkerze
(to) **speak** *(irr)*	sprechen; reden
special	besondere(r, s); besonders
species (*pl* **species**)	(die) Art; (die) Spezies
spectacular	atemberaubend; spektakulär
spelling	(das) Buchstabieren; (die) Rechtschreibung
(to) **spend** *(irr)*	verbringen *(Zeit)*; ausgeben *(Geld)*
spider	(die) Spinne
sport	(der) Sport; (die) Sportart
(to) **do sports** *(irr)*	Sport treiben
spring	(der) Frühling
squirrel	(das) Eichhörnchen
stadium	(das) Stadion
stage	(die) Bühne
stair	(die) Stufe
stairs *(pl)*	(die) Treppe
stall	(der) Stand
(to) **stand** *(irr)*	stehen
(to) **stand for** *(irr)*	stehen für
(to) **start**	anfangen; beginnen
station	(die) U-Bahn-Station; (der) Bahnhof
(to) **stay**	bleiben; wohnen
(to) **stay out**	ausbleiben, wegbleiben

snake

a pair of **socks**

sparkler

stairs

step	(die) Stufe; (der) Schritt
(to) **step**	treten; steigen
stick	(der) Stock
(to) **stick to** *(irr)*	*hier:* sich halten an
still	(immer) noch
stone	(der) Stein
(to) **stop**	aufhören
story	(die) Geschichte, (die) Erzählung
straight on	geradeaus
strange	sonderbar; merkwürdig
(to) **stream**	streamen
street	(die) Straße
stress	(die) Betonung
strict	streng
string	(die) Schnur; (die) Kordel
student	(der) Schüler / (die) Schülerin
stuff *(informal)*	(das) Zeug
stupid	dumm, blöd
style	(der) Stil
such	so; solch
suddenly	plötzlich
sugar	(der) Zucker
summer	(der) Sommer
summer camp	(das) Sommercamp
sun cream	(die) Sonnenschutzcreme
Sunday	(der) Sonntag
sunny	sonnig
sunset	(der) Sonnenuntergang
sure	sicher
surface	(die) Oberfläche
surprised	überrascht; erstaunt
sweet	(die) Süßigkeit
(to) **swim** *(irr)*	schwimmen
(to) **go swimming** *(irr)*	schwimmen gehen
swimming	(das) Schwimmen
swimming pool	(das) Schwimmbad
(to) **switch off**	ausschalten
syllable	(die) Silbe

stick

string

a **sweet** shop

T

table	(der) Tisch
tablespoon	(der) Esslöffel
(to) **take** *(irr)*	nehmen; bringen
(to) **take a photo** *(irr)*	ein Foto machen
(to) **take a picture** *(irr)*	ein Foto machen
(to) **take a ride** *(irr)*	*hier:* Karussell fahren
(to) **take care of** *(irr)*	sich kümmern um

The boy is setting the **table**.

(to) **take off** *(irr)*	ausziehen *(Kleidung)*
(to) **take out** *(irr)*	hinausbringen
(to) **take part in** *(irr)*	teilnehmen an
(to) **talk about**	sprechen über
(to) **talk (to)**	sprechen (mit); reden (mit)
tall	groß
tapas *(pl)*	*(die) spanischen Appetithäppchen*
target task	(die) Zielaufgabe
teacher	(der) Lehrer / (die) Lehrerin
technology	(die) Technologie; (die) Technik
telephone	(das) Telefon
(to) **tell** *(irr)*	erzählen
terrible, terribly	schrecklich
(to) **text**	eine Textnachricht schreiben
text (message)	(die) Textnachricht
Thames	(die) Themse
than	als *(bei Vergleich)*
thank God	Gott sei Dank
thank you, thanks	danke
that	das; der/die/das (dort); dass; so
that's (= **that is**)	das ist
the	der/die/das
theatre	(das) Theater
their	ihr(e)
them	sie; ihnen
then	dann
there	dort; dahin
these (*pl of* **this**)	diese; das
they	sie
thing	(das) Ding; (der) Gegenstand
(to) **think** *(irr)*	denken; glauben
(to) **think about** *(irr)*	denken an, nachdenken über
(to) **think of** *(irr)*	denken an, sich ausdenken
this	diese(r, s)
this way	hier entlang
those (*pl of* **that**)	diese, jene
thousand	tausend
through	durch
(to) **throw** *(irr)*	werfen
Thursday	(der) Donnerstag
(to) **tidy (up)**	aufräumen
tie	(die) Krawatte
time	(die) Zeit; (das) Mal
tip	(der) Tipp
tired	müde
title	(der) Titel; (die) Überschrift
to	in; nach; zu; an; (um) zu; bis; für

teacher

taller größer
the tallest am größten; der/die/das größte

there is / there are dort ist / dort sind; es gibt
there was / there were dort war / waren; es gab
there will be es wird geben
there won't be es wird nicht geben
there's (= **there is**) dort ist; es gibt

tie

all the time die ganze Zeit
at this time zu dieser Zeit
for the first time zum ersten Mal
on time pünktlich

today	heute; heutzutage
toffee apple	*(der) kandierte Apfel*
together	zusammen
toilet	(die) Toilette
toilet paper	(das) Toilettenpapier
tomorrow	morgen
tonight	heute Abend
too	auch; zu
top	(das) obere Ende; (die) Spitze
torch (*pl* **torches**)	(die) Taschenlampe
(to) **touch**	berühren
towards	in Richtung, zu; gegenüber
tower	(der) Turm
town	(die) Stadt
train	(der) Zug
trainer	(der) Turnschuh
transport	(der) Transport; Verkehrsmittel
travel	(die) Reise
(to) **travel**	reisen; fahren
treason	(der) (Landes)verrat
tree	(der) Baum
Trick or treat!	*etwa: Süßes oder es gibt Saures!*
trick-or-treating	*(das) Spiel zu Halloween, bei dem die Kinder von Tür zu Tür gehen und entweder Süßigkeiten bekommen oder einen Streich spielen*
trip	(der) Ausflug; (die) Fahrt
trouble	(der) Ärger; (die) Schwierigkeiten
(a pair of) trousers	(die) Hose
true	wahr
(to) **try**	(aus)probieren; versuchen
the Tube	(die) (Londoner) U-Bahn
Tuesday	(der) Dienstag
Turkish	türkisch
(to) **turn**	abbiegen
TV (= television)	(das) Fernsehen; (der) Fernseher
(to) **watch TV**	Fernsehen gucken
twin	(der) Zwilling; Zwillings-
type	(die) Art
typical	typisch

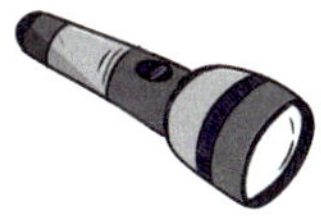

torch

train

tree

(to) **be in trouble** in Schwierigkeiten sein

(to) **get into trouble** in Schwierigkeiten geraten

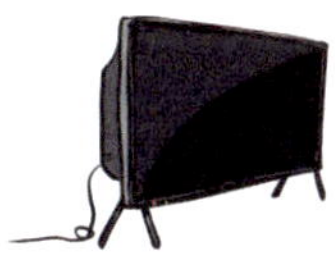

TV

U

the UK (= United Kingdom)	(das) Vereinigte Königreich
uncle	(der) Onkel
until	bis
up	nach oben; hinauf; oben
up to	bis (zu)

us	uns
the USA (= United States of America)	(die) USA; (die) Vereinigten Staaten von Amerika
(to) **use**	benutzen
useful	nützlich
usually	gewöhnlich; normalerweise

V

vegetarian	(der) Vegetarier / (die) Vegetarierin; vegetarisch
vehicle	(das) Fahrzeug
version	(die) Version, (die) Fassung
very	sehr
vet	(der) Tierarzt / (die) Tierärztin
via	über
view	(die) (Aus)sicht
violin	(die) Violine; (die) Geige
virtual	virtuell
visit	(der) Besuch
(to) **visit**	besuchen
visitor	(der) Besucher / (die) Besucherin
VR (= virtual reality)	(die) virtuelle Realität

He is a **very** good teacher.
Er ist ein sehr guter Lehrer.
I like him **very much**.
Ich mag ihn sehr.

visitors

W

(to) **wait**	(er)warten
(to) **wake up** *(irr)*	aufwachen
(to) **wake somebody up** *(irr)*	jemanden aufwecken
walk	(der) Spaziergang; (der) Weg
(to) **walk**	gehen
(to) **walk on**	weiterlaufen
walking	(das) Wandern
walkway	(der) (Fuß)weg
wall	(die) Wand
walrus (*pl* **walrus** *or* **walruses**)	(das) Walross
(to) **want** (to)	wollen
(to) **wash**	waschen; sich waschen
(to) **watch**	beobachten; ansehen
watch	(die) (Armband)uhr
(to) **watch out**	aufpassen
(to) **watch TV**	Fernsehen gucken
water	(das) Wasser
wax model	(das) Wachsmodell
way	(der) Weg; (die) Art
we	wir
(to) **wear** *(irr)*	tragen *(Kleidung)*
weather	(das) Wetter

walk

I **was** ich war
he / she / it **was** er / sie / es war

this way hier entlang

we'd (= we would) wir würden
we'll (= we will) wir werden

Wednesday	(der) Mittwoch
week	(die) Woche
weekend	(das) Wochenende
at the weekend	am Wochenende
(to) **weigh**	wiegen
weight	(das) Gewicht
(to) **welcome**	willkommen heiβen
well	gut; nun
well done	gut gemacht
Welsh	walisisch
what	was; welche(r, s)
when	wann; wenn; als
where	wo; wohin
which	welche(r, s); was
white	weiβ
who	wer; der/die/das
whole	ganz, gesamt
why	warum
wide	weit
wife (*pl* **wives**)	(die) Ehefrau
wildlife	(die) Tier- und Pflanzenwelt
will	werden
winter	(der) Winter
with	mit; bei
without	ohne
woman (*pl* **women**)	(die) Frau
won't	nicht werden
(to) **wonder**	sich fragen
wonderful	wunderbar, wundervoll
wood	(das) Holz
wooden	Holz-, hölzern
word	(das) Wort
word search	(die) Wortsuche
(to) **work**	arbeiten; funktionieren
work	(die) Arbeit; (das) Werk
all the work	die ganze Arbeit
world	(die) Welt
all over the world	auf der ganzen Welt
worried	beunruhigt, besorgt
(to) **worry**	sich Sorgen machen
worse	schlechter, schlimmer
the worst	der/die/das schlechteste/ schlimmste; am schlechtesten/ schlimmsten
would	würde(st, n, t)
(to) **wrap**	einwickeln
(to) **write** *(irr)*	schreiben

An elephant **weighs** a lot.

Welcome to ...!
Willkommen in ...!

you **were** du warst / ihr wart
we **were** wir waren
they **were** sie waren

What about ...? Was ist mit ...? / Wie wäre es mit ...?
What about you? Und du?
What is it about? Worum geht es?
What is it like? Wie ist es?
What was that like? Wie war das?
what's (= what is) was ist
What's going on? Was passiert gerade?
What's on? *(informal)* Was ist los?

wood 

Don't worry.
Mach dir keine Sorgen.

I would like ... (= I'd like ...)
Ich würde gern ... /
Ich hätte gern ...
He / She would like ...
Er / Sie würde gern ... /
Er / Sie hätte gern ...

wrong	falsch

X

xxx (= kisses) *(informal)*	*(die) Küsschen (am Ende eines informellen Briefes oder einer Nachricht)*

Y

year	(das) Jahr; (das) Schuljahr; (die) Klasse
all year round	das ganze Jahr lang
yes	ja
yesterday	gestern
you	du; dich; dir; man; ihr; euch; Sie; Ihnen
young	jung
your	dein(e); euer/eure; Ihr(e)
yours	deine(r, s); eure(r, s); Ihre(r, s)
yours sincerely	mit freundlichen Grüßen *(am Ende eines formellen Briefes)*
yourself	dir, dich; sich
youth club	(der) Jugendklub
yummy *(informal)*	lecker

Yes, I have. Ja.
Yes, it does. Ja.
Yes, it is. Ja.
Yes, you can. Ja.

you're (= you are) du bist, ihr seid

younger jüngere(r, s)
the youngest der/die/das jüngste

Z

zoo	(der) Zoo
zoologist	(der) Zoologe / (die) Zoologin